# RAISE 'EM RIGHT

## POSITIVE PARENTING
## FOR SINGLE MOTHERS

Kimm Reid-Matchett, BA (Psy)

cover design by Tamara Yingst (yingst@shaw.ca)

PublishAmerica
Baltimore

First printing

PublishAmerica has allowed this work to remain exactly as the author intended, verbatim, without editorial input.

ISBN: 978-1-4489-4948-9
PUBLISHED BY PUBLISHAMERICA, LLLP
www.publishamerica.com
Baltimore

Printed in the United States of America

# Dedication

I am deeply blessed to have so many fantastic and supportive people in my life. There is no way I would have made it through the dark hours of my journey without my friends and family lifting me up and my saviour carrying me. First, my precious children; Riley, Jesse, and Brady. Thank you so much for having enough patience to let me learn and enough grace to forgive my mistakes. You are absolutely the lights of my life and I am eternally in love with you. You are my pride and my joy. Forever and always. To my husband Scott, thank you for putting up with my annoying chatter and constant over analyzing. You have encouraged me and have more faith in my ability than I ever will. I love you. Finally to my parents. You have been with me on every crazy twist and turn on this journey and I am forever grateful for your prayers and your blessing. You have never turned me away and I know above all that you are always on my side, cheering me on, and I am blessed beyond measure because I have you in my life. Thank you. Finally, to my Jesus Christ who has carried me when I was too weak to walk, who has allowed me to learn from my mistakes and who has surrounded me with amazing people. Eternally yours.

# Table of Contents

# Foreword

Single parenting is not for the fainthearted, the frail, the impatient, or the perfectionist. Raising children alone is without a doubt one of life's most challenging yet rewarding journeys. Such a journey guarantees an unpredictable path that winds down, down, down through its deepest darkest valleys overrun with dense, prickly, nearly impassable brush.

This same path turns and wanders upward to find freedoms and blessings amidst the rolling mountains, blinding sunshine, and unimaginable beauty. It is there we find ourselves standing on the highest peaks far above the billowing clouds, realizing all that Christ has done for us along the journey.

This journey unveils desperately lonely times when we are sure our heart and soul will crumble like the ashes from the fire pit we roasted our marshmallows over the night before. There are times of pure heavenly blessing when our spirits leap within us and we experience the joy the Bible refers to as "unspeakable and full of glory."

I understand these times far too well because I have walked, stumbled, and blindly crawled along this ever turning, unpredictable path from the glory of the heavens to the darkness of the valleys, round and round, and back again. In fact, if you come across a few spots where the path is well watered and the trees are lush and the grass is green, those are the places where my tears watered the ground well. If you see other places where the path is nearly worn through, it's because I have trod it far too many times.

On this path of single motherhood, I have learned who my God is. I have lived daily in His strength when my own was diminished to a heap of rubble. I have learned to walk in His joy, regardless of the circumstances that surrounded me, often threatening to devour me. I have learned to run and dance in the freedom and joy that He graciously gives.

He has painstakingly taught me to enjoy the little things and not worry about those things which I am powerless to change. He has blessed me with understanding and wisdom. He has covered me with His care and gently placed me on the wings of mighty eagles so that I might soar above the path and rest with Him awhile, enjoying His presence.

Although I continue to journey on the path, it's a bit softer because He is with me, sustaining me with His peace. Once in a while, I still stumble over the bigger blockades, but He never lets me fall. As I stand at the edge of the cliff where the path becomes terrifying and treacherous, I am thankful that He has kept me from falling—or jumping.

It is my deepest pleasure to walk with you on this path and welcome you to a brief moment of rest on the journey. I pray I can steer you clear of the blockades and boulders along the path I wish had been pointed out to me; instead, I hit them head on and suffered the consequences they brought. I hope that as you open the cover and dive in, you will find laughter, compassion, understanding, and the divine wisdom of God's Word to light your path.

# Introduction

Single parenting. The words cause our hair to stand on end. They can invoke sheer terror. Just yesterday I had someone say to me, "Those single moms—I just don't know how they do it." I had to agree.

How does one person obtain all that is required to raise children? Money, wisdom, grace, discipline, tenacity, answers, reasoning abilities, the ability to go for days without proper sleep and still maintain sanity, and the list goes on. Who can possibly single-handedly do the job that God designed for two people to accomplish?

Simply maintaining a daily schedule can be mind-boggling. But as moms we must look at more than just the daily schedule. If we want children to grow into respectful, self-disciplined, healthy, responsible members of society, we must do much more than simply check off a series of "to-do's" listed on a crumpled coffee-stained scrap of paper.

In order to empower our children to dwell safely and positively in society, we must listen to them, instill values and virtues into their minds, nurture their spirits, and discipline their failures. We must pick which battles to fight and which ones to ignore. We must teach and facilitate consistency and positivity. We can choose to just squeak through the day without losing our minds but this will not give us—or our children—the outcomes we all desire.

Instead, we must choose to give it our all, giving up much of ourselves in order to accomplish our goal. We must pull up our socks, put our noses to the grindstone, jump in with both feet (I could go on all day with these tacky-over-the-top sayings), and put some elbow grease into it.

Seriously though, it takes the peace that passes all understanding and the wisdom of God our Father. Christ says in James 1:5 that if we are lacking wisdom, we can come to Him and ask in faith, and if we trust Him, He *will* give us that necessary wisdom. And He does—always.

What you will find on these pages is a small bit of that wisdom He gave to me when I was in desperate need and fell to the floor on my face and asked Him. I now pass it onto you to apply to your own situation so that you too may take great joy and pride in raising excellent children for His glory and your pride.

I am proud of my children and I know that if you apply these principles to your own family you will have the great and blessed opportunity to be proud of your children.

# Section One—Discovering My Value

Zephaniah 3:17 says, "The Lord your God is with you, he is mighty to save. He will take great delight in you, he will quiet you with his love, he will rejoice over you with singing."

You are valuable. You may not feel like you are, but you are more valuable than a shiny red ruby or a sparkling diamond. After you have walked a few miles on the rocky path of single parenthood, you will likely not feel too special, but rest assured, you are a prized possession.

El Shaddai, the maker of heaven and earth, He who commands the lightning where to strike and knows the name of every star and even when one is missing, thinks you are more valuable than anything else in this world. He looks at you and smiles and shouts, "That's my girl." He is proud of you and wants to know you more. He is calling you to come to Him and listen. Listen to Him who sings of your beauty, your radiance, and your value. Listen to Him who beams with pride over you. Listen to Him who knows everything about you, every thought in your head, every hurt, every sadness, every regret, and loves you regardless. Just listen.

# YOU'RE NOT ALONE

My life began as many of yours did—cold, naked, and screaming. I am quite seriously considering going out the same way I came in, but only time will determine my grand exit. I was born during a blizzard, as the middle child to wonderful Christian parents and part of a large farming family. I was taken to bible camp and Sunday school since the time of my conception, so I knew very well all the right things to do and say, what to wear and what was completely unacceptable attire on any given Sunday morning.

I quickly learned that sitting on the front pew conveniently three rows ahead of my parents was not the time to clean the bottoms of my new shoes with spit and the hem of my skirt. Apparently this was not allowed in church, and was in fact absolutely forbidden. I had strict but loving parents who wanted nothing but the very best for me, and did everything in their power to ensure my safety and well being.

I was a typical young tomboyish farm girl. Being born during a blizzard may have had an impact on my ability to reason and possibly jeopardized any common sense I might otherwise have had. I had enormous dreams of growing up quickly, getting married, and having a dozen children.

My Prince Charming was going to come marching in from somewhere only found in fairy tales, sweep me off my feet, carry me far away (preferably no farther than the vacant lot next door to my parents), and spoil me rotten. He was going to adore me and lavish amazingly expensive gifts on me. We'd have a dozen adorable, perfect little children who would grow up as happy and perfectly well adjusted as I had. They would *never* clean the bottoms of their shoes with dresses or ties while sitting on the front pew of church. That much I knew.

That was my blonde hair, blue eyed childhood dream. My reality, on the other hand, was to turn out much differently than my fairy tale. Long before I ever had a chance to grow up or even get comfortable with puberty and boobs, I met my Prince Charming. He didn't come from anywhere unknown or amazing; he came from the high school classroom marked 12D just down the hall from my 10B classroom.

Not surprisingly, this would prove to be a downfall for my studies. I never quite managed to pass basic math in high school, simply because numbers seem to have a tendency to get lost somewhere between my frontal lobe and my hypothalamus. It didn't help that Prince Charming had a free class which conveniently coincided with Math 101. That 2:15 class quickly became secondary and consequently my instructor never knew that my name had a face until interview time. My report card said simply, "This student may pass basic math if she would consider attending class."

This may come as a surprise, but that statement became a household joke which still follows me today. After all, who needs math to marry Prince Charming and have a dozen babies? Perhaps if someone is actually having a dozen children, a sex education class may be beneficial, but certainly not math.

Obviously, I was in a state of extreme naivety and never even considered that I might one day *not* live with prince charming. I certainly made no effort or plan to enable me to look after myself—or my future children—if something should happen. After all, that sort of thing was not going to happen to me. It was simply not part of my life's plan.

Boy, can I be wrong sometimes! Once in a while, my mistakes are embarrassing, and often they cost me something: pride, money, an apology. However, my lack of planning and thought for the future mixed in with my over-the-top trust-everybody-never-think-poorly-of-anybody naivety cost me enormously this time.

Now, please don't get me wrong. I am not saying, implying, or even slightly suggesting that marrying Prince Charming straight out of high school without getting a diploma, a job, or a clue was a mistake. I am not saying that at all—but I wouldn't recommend it.

My mistake was simply being so blinded by teenage love, a gorgeous snow white wedding gown, and the idealistic concept of being a wife that I failed to plan for anything different or take a look at any other options in life.

Getting married so young was not particularly intelligent, although I know many who have and it has worked out wonderfully. Believing my life would be very similar to those dearly loved fairy tale princesses was somewhat shallow and unrealistic.

Being married shortly out of high school didn't work in our favour, and neither was the fact that we came from two very opposite backgrounds. I said white; he said I'm color blind. I am creative; he is not. He is athletic; I'm a klutz. I wanted a dozen children; he wanted a couple. (Who knew that ten wasn't a good compromise?) I grew up in church; he grew up in the hockey rink. He is very smart; I'm not the sharpest tool in the shed. I never had a paying job when I was in school; he bought his own car by tenth grade. I lived a very sheltered childhood; he did not. Get the picture? Complete opposites in every area imaginable. Neither of our backgrounds, skills, or abilities were wrong; they were just different.

By the time we'd been married about six years, we had two wonderful sons. I attended secretarial school, got a diploma, and worked in a bible school office in order to help fund my husband's education. He did well and graduated at the top of his class. After seven years, I ended up moving out of the home with my two small sons. As many moms in theses circumstances do, I moved into my parents' home for a time. I need to honour and acknowledge my parents. They have definitely walked with me on my journey and have paved a few miles of my rocky, twisted path. Where they couldn't pave it, they prayed that I'd make it through.

Much to their dismay, it was on their wedding anniversary when I showed up on their doorstep with two sons; one in diapers with snot running down his face and much too young to understand the upcoming trauma, the other only four years old...just old enough to be affected by the daily turmoil, but not quite old enough to understand or know which questions to ask.

I read books, I studied, I prayed—a lot. You see, I was on welfare and could afford two things—rent and food. Nothing else. Not a movie, not furniture, not clothing, nothing. Someone lent me a couch and my dear grandmother let me borrow her kitchen table, but that was it. I had a small television, but could not afford cable so there was really no purpose for the television other than to set my coffee cup on.

When one has two small children who go to bed by 7:00 pm, and absolutely nothing else to do after that time, and just happens to be in a serious crisis, one spends a significant amount of time praying. It was in this little house with no furniture, no friends, no phone, and no television that I met and fell in love with Jesus. His Holy Spirit hovered in that house and I learned things that would prove to become my lifeline many times over.

Maybe because I found peace of mind and heart, or maybe because my husband was getting lonely, I can't really say, but he started coming to visit us. He would simply come to play with the boys for an hour or so and end up staying long after they were asleep. After a couple months of this, we moved back home. Sadly, things did not improve once we were all under the same roof again. As commonly happens, our circumstances became worse—much worse.

Desperate, lonely, and heart-broken, I fell at the foot of my saviour. I begged Him to help me, to pull me out of the pit I found myself in, and to shine His light into the small hole I was squinting through. Anything to see a glimmer of hope—the tinniest light. I felt very deeply that as long as I had unrest about leaving the relationship, I was to stay in it and fight for its healing; so I did. Everyday I would beg God to either let me out, give me that desired peace about leaving, or bring changes into my home. Everyday I heard the same thing. "You are there for a purpose. I will give you rest and keep you safe, but you cannot leave." So I stayed.

It was during this time of desperately seeking the saviour that I truly found Him. Yes, He was with me in that little house I'd had before returning home, and He taught me so much. Now, however, I had to trust Him in the midst of the circumstances. What He showed me was His peace, which goes beyond any human understanding. I felt His arms firmly around me, loving me when I believed I was unlovable. I heard His voice caress my heart and heal it. I found His love, which is unending and inseparable. I obeyed Him and stayed in the relationship. And just like He said He would, He provided everything I needed.

Then it happened. After many years of pain and heartache, I was simply standing in my kitchen watching a coin twirl and spin on the table. As I stood there, I heard my Saviour's voice. "My precious daughter, I give you peace—you are free to go."

Now, I'm not a theologian, and I realize that many people reading those words are not going to agree. They might even say the voice I heard was not God. I know differently, though, and if you've been in similar situations, you know differently too. I don't know why God asked me to stay in the situation for five years if He was going to eventually let me out of it. What I do know is that I met my Saviour and on that day He rescued me.

I got my wits about me and a few days later I had a conversation with my husband. I told him matter-of-factly that we needed a drastic and immediate change to stop the cycle that was going on in our family. We had three small boys and we could not keep passing down the generational cycles of craziness. He agreed and we decided to go our separate ways.

I knew for certain a few things. First, I had no education, not even a high school diploma. I ran a daycare in my home, but I knew the measly income I took from it was not going to cover many of the bills, let alone the mortgage. Second, I was solely responsible for the emotional, physical, and mental well being of three wide-eyed, innocent little boys. Finally, I knew that my God would never leave me or forsake me. Times were going to be tough, but my faith in God was deeper than my fear and panic. He would be with me every step of this twisted and rocky journey.

For the next year, I struggled desperately to keep our home. I was babysitting way too many children and was physically and emotionally drained. I could not afford milk for my babies or my coffee, which is what I lived on for the first year. In fact, when my neighbours would pop by for a steaming cup of yesterdays nuked coffee, they'd bring their own milk because they knew I would not have any. My friends would pop by and fill my fridge with some necessities and often a few luxuries as well. "There was a big sale," they would try convincing me. "I could not pass it by and I already have some."

I literally could not afford shoes for my children that first summer. There were many necessities that we were learning to live without, but God never left. My family had attended a bible camp for many, many years and I desperately wanted to attend with my sons. They had many friends there and I knew it would be great for their wounded little spirits, but I certainly didn't have money for that sort of thing. My poverty was painfully heavy and I was beginning to slouch under the weight of it.

I recall having to sell my little camper in order to pay for my vehicle maintenance bills just so I could have a road-worthy car. Often, when my boys were visiting their father, I'd work extra jobs here and there just to make enough money to pay the minimum payments on the most desperate of my bills. It was a deep, deep well and there was certainly no way I was going to crawl out of it short of a miracle. Fortunately, I serve a God who is a miracle worker, which gave me just enough hope to get up each morning and carry on.

I did get to camp that summer, and every summer since. The director phoned me during one of the short stints my phone was connected, and gave me great news. Someone had donated enough funding to cover our costs and we were invited to attend that year completely free of charge. God provides.

I am so excited about how good God is and for all His provisions. One thing I have learned is that there is a large difference between wants and needs. I have learned to live without wants, and I have learned that God doesn't always agree with the things I I consider needs. Sometimes we think we need a vehicle when all we really need is a ride. God always provides the rides, but He may not provide the vehicle.

As I was packing to leave for camp, pleading with God, trying to make a case for shoes being a need that He was supposed to provide, one of my cousins stopped by. She often popped in for a quick visit and to check up on me. She always had a jug or two of milk and a couple loaves of bread to sneak into my fridge. That day, she had something extra in her bag—summer shoes for my sons. I recently spoke to her about those shoes, but she had long forgotten. I never will.

She never once made me feel embarrassed or that I owed her. Cindy just sweetly put those little shoes on my boys' feet and said she had found a great sale and just couldn't pass it by; her kids all had new shoes, so they didn't need any. "The shoes were so cute that I just had to buy them and then think of who I could give them to," she said. She made it seem as if I'd done her a favour by having three little boys with dirty, shoeless feet so that she had someone to give those shoes to. Thanks, Cindy. I'm forever grateful—you have been a blessing more times than you know!

Since that time, many years ago, God has allowed me to walk the journey with Him. I have lost friends and gained weight. I've parented alone for long periods of time and had long periods of time when I've been alone and desperately sad beyond measure, but God has never left my side.

I've been able to bond deeply with my sons, raise them to know and love God, and journey with them. I have blessed them and been blessed by them. As they've gotten older, they have chosen, one by one, to try living with their father and I have had to smile, hold my chin up, and support that. Watching them pack their little bags to move to daddy's for a time has brought more pain than I thought I could handle. Those days ripped my heart out, stomped on it, threw it through the shredder, and stuffed it back into my chest, yet I supported my sons' decisions because, after all, they love their father as much as they love me.

When my oldest son turned fourteen he chose to live with his father who lived an hour away. We lived in a small town and he wanted to go to a big high school. Keep in mind that I was the mom who sat in the bleachers not only for the games but also for the practices. I was the mom who did the driving and who had a van of nine other boys because the other parents had plans, were busy, or simply didn't want go to the exhausting tournaments every weekend. Now my son was gone and it tore me to pieces.

For months and even years, I'd sit on his bed and smell his blankets and my heart would bleed with pain. It was worse than death in my mind and it is certainly not something one gets used to.

I had to come to grips with the fact that these boys were not choosing him over me, nor were they ditching me for him. They were being young men who wanted to build a relationship with their father, and I had to respect that and love them enough to let them.

There are times on my journey when I thought about dying, when I begged God to close the door on my journey and open the pearly gates so that I could be free of pain. I have teetered between depression and simply not caring. I've wondered if the corner bar had any peace to offer and I've pondered simply disappearing. But every time, without exception, at the point I thought I could take no more, God showed up. He scoops me up and loves on me, reassures me that He will never leave me nor forsake me, and He gives me strength for all things.

Along my journey, I have experienced nearly every imaginable pain that coexists with being a single mother and my heart has broken for my children—and myself—time after time. I can dry their tears, but I cannot heal their wounds. However, I know someone who can, and He can heal your wounds if you let Him.

I know scarring pain, and I know God's peace. One cannot survive the pain without experiencing the peace and knowing the peacemaker deeply and intimately. It has been said that when we fall, God picks us up, wipes us off, and sets us up again to keep going. After falling time and time again, I know differently.

I know that when we fall, God doesn't just pick us up and set us back down to try again. My God picks us up and snuggles us tightly to Himself. He doesn't wipe us off, but rather He bathes us completely in His peace and love, putting brand new spotless garments on us. He doesn't just set us right back onto the path, but instead absolutely loves on us until we are strong enough and ready to be gently set down.

So please allow me to journey with you. I have been where you are—and I have been where you are going. I can tell you that although it is hard, everything turns out okay. I am walking with you, but someone so much better is right there along-side as well. Let Christ shine his light on the path so you might avoid many of the pitfalls, rocks, and jagged edges. Believe me, you are not alone.

# GOOD RIDDANCE TO BAD RUBBISH

Rubbish: something that is considered to have—or has—no value.

After spending significant time talking to parents, I firmly believe that for the most part, parents want the very best for their children. Regrettably, we don't always manage to successfully achieve "the best" and some of us screw up far more than others; but in our heart of hearts, we all want to raise great kids. I have yet to find a mother who looked me in the eye and said with an evil grin, "I intentionally want to ruin my children and ensure they have no chance at an enjoyable and prosperous future."

What I often do find are moms who reveal an intense desire to raise children who are kind and respectful, able to make good decisions, and able to accept consequences when they make bad decisions—children who will not be forever damaged by their circumstances or lack of a full-time father. Unfortunately, such an ability to raise these wonderful, unwounded children is not some magical internal wisdom that we are born with. We are not born with an inner knowledge to always make the right decisions or follow through on the decisions that we have made for our children. We parent, for the most part, how we were parented. It is learned behaviour, not instinctual. If you happened to be born to wise and balanced people, then you are fortunate and you probably learned very good parenting skills. Just as the positive is true, so is the negative.

Nevertheless, we all have space to learn and grow, make up for past mistakes and do exponentially better in the future. Moms, it is possible to empower and raise excellent children, regardless of our circumstances, if we set our eyes on Christ—the eternally perfect parent.

When we fail to enlist Christ as our every-minute-of-the-day connection, our personal views of life easily become fuzzy and we end up trying to see clearly through dirty lenses. This is obviously difficult, if not impossible; seeing clearly through dirt is quite a conundrum! It is even more difficult and potentially damaging when we think our lenses are clean when in fact they are etched and full of grime.

Often, we have spent so much time looking through the thick muck that we convince ourselves that untruth is truth and masks are genuine. We see things as we wish them to be, not as they really are.

There is not a person alive who has not looked through dirty lenses at one time or another in their lives. Where does the muck and grime come from? From hurt. From rejection. From failure. From sin—sometimes our sin and sometimes the sin of others. Everyone who breathes has experienced the jagged daggers of hurt and pain. It is inevitable, however, and sometimes the hurt seems more than we can bear.

Countless numbers of individuals, who are now parents, have grown up in damaging circumstances of all different sorts. Whether physical violence, verbal or mental abuse, sexual abuse or even spiritual abuse, it all hurts and the scars are absolutely irreparable. The wounds can heal, but the scars will remain.

These particular circumstances, of course, are the most damaging, always leaving a plethora of unanswered questions. These abuses damage not only the physical body, but mental and emotional areas as well. The wounds end up severely muddying our lenses, often making life a treacherous journey.

There are countless types of hurts, other than those already mentioned. They may be less dirty, but dirty nonetheless.

Regardless of the circumstances that have etched and muddied our lenses, the fact is that we cannot see clearly. That is where the blood of Jesus can wash the filth away, empowering us with a clear and truthful vision for our future, and that of our children.

Childhood can bring with it feelings of rejection and blame, fear and bitterness. We bring all these wounds into our adulthood and through them our own parenting styles and abilities are developed. No one is completely sheltered from negative memories of childhood because, of course, we have all been children and we have all had imperfect parents.

Regardless of how healthy and safe our own childhood homes may have been, free from abuse, rejection or hardship, nobody gets through unscathed. You may have grown up in a very healthy home with an unending supply of love and acceptance, perfectly balanced with effective discipline, but somewhere you were hurt. Maybe on the playground or in school or out behind Aunt Tilly's woodshed. Let's face it—we've all been hurt. It is the cycle of life as long as we live here on this earth.

If your childhood was the one that was perfect, with mom and dad both home and loving perfectly—and you were fortunate enough to have loving, kind and compassionate siblings, don't kid yourself. That peaceful bliss likely did not carry on without any glitches. Life just doesn't work that way. Believe me, I wish it did.

Adult life hits and the world we now live in is much different than that of our parents'. With the blessing of technology—computers, continual internet access, internet dating, MSN, Facebook, cell phones, iPods, etc.—comes the curse of technology. They are one in the same.

Twenty years ago, an affair was an affair. The lines were black and white. Today we have managed to successfully manufacture a grey area. Is it really considered an affair if it's only online? What if the two never meet face to face? Isn't it just a harmless fantasy? Innocent fun?

Families are breaking up at lightning speed and, in fact, just this morning my eyes landed on a Facebook post which read, "Will a week ever go by that I don't hear of another marriage breaking down?" "Probably not," was my response.

Life is hard. Nowhere in the Word of God does He promise a life of harmony, ease, and peace. He does promise that He will be our peace amidst turbulent times and He promises never to leave us regardless of our circumstances. He will most certainly walk with us while we go through the dark times, but He never suggests that those dark times won't come.

They came for Paul when he was shipwrecked and beaten and stoned and imprisoned. They came for Jonah in the belly of the fish (I'm not entirely certain which would have been more dark for Jonah—being swallowed or being regurgitated onto the shore). They came for Mary as she watched her precious little boy being crucified. Hard times will come. Thank God that is not the end of the story. It's only the beginning.

Hard times offer us opportunity to trust God. We can never fully experience the fullness of joy if we have never felt the empty ache of sorrow. We won't understand the contentment of peace if we've never walked in unrest. We cannot know the release of forgiveness until we've been released by forgiveness. God is so absolutely, unequivocally brilliant!

By now, I hope the point has been undeniably made that we *all* have experienced pain and sorrow. I'm going to assume (I know that is a dangerous thing to do, but I'm going to step out and do it anyway) that you are either a single mother or you know someone who is. I can safely assume such a thing because you are reading this book. I'm going to take that assumption one step further (brave, aren't I?) and say the chances that you have been hurt in the relationship with your child's father are fairly high. And finally, I will throw in the chance that you still hold, at least to some extent, resentment, bitterness, or deep hurt.

Okay, so we have all been hurt—that's been identified. The question now becomes what to do about it. It is absolutely impossible to positively parent and empower our children if we have not dealt with our own hurts. We cannot continue to look through lenses that are etched, muddied, or charred and expect to see our children's needs clearly. We cannot model positivity if we have a negative attitude. Certainly, teaching forgiveness when we model resentment is going to be difficult, and expecting acceptance when we fear rejection is going to be impossible.

In order to unconditionally love our children the way they need to be loved and raise them how they deserve to be raised, we must be able to gaze truthfully into our own lives and come face to face with our own "stuff." There are many things that can fit into our "stuff" box, so we must initially decide what is ours—what we are holding onto—and then determine to grab it out of our "stuff" box and firmly put it down.

It can be difficult to put down something we have been holding on to and hiding behind. Often, this "stuff" has become our identity. We have learned how to hide behind it, live within it, and disregard it as the driving force within ourselves. The truth is that our identity is in Christ, not in our "stuff," and it is absolutely crucial that we exchange our faulty identity for the identity that is found in Christ alone.

"Forget the former things; do not dwell on the past. See, I am doing a new thing! Now it springs up; do you not perceive it? I am making a way in the desert and streams in the wasteland" (Isaiah 43:18-19).

The Word of God says it clearly—the truth will set you free. The truth is that we are not what our circumstances try to make us or who our wounds tell us we are. We are more; we are competent, we are able, we are complete, and we are eternally and perfectly loved. 2 Corinthians 4:8 suggests that we are queens and princesses because the Lord has in store for us a crown of righteousness which He—God Almighty—will award to us. I certainly don't mind being God's princess, do you?

We can safely put down the rubbish, even if we feel like it owns us. We can exchange it for the truth of God, our Father. In order to be all that we want to be, we must have a solid foundational identity. The only place to get that identity is in Christ and His Word. We are *not* what nosey neighbours say we are, we are *not* who the gossiping ladies in the back row of church suppose us to be, and we are certainly *not* worth what the banker who's trying to get a loan payment out of our empty account assumes us to be worth.

Moms, our children are going to be childish at times and our teenagers are going to be self-centered and moody. That's just the way it is, but if we take those common everyday age appropriate behaviours as a personal attack, we are going to be distraught most of the time. No one can parent well from behind such enormous walls, so step out from behind them and experience life on the other side—a life of acceptance, joy, and freedom.

Most often, stepping out from behind our self-erected walls will require forgiving those who have hurt us, and changing our belief system from one that says, "I am a nobody, a failure, invaluable," to one of "I am a daughter of the most high God and He loves me unconditionally all the way to the cross—I must be incredibly important to the King if He loves me so much."

It is like a container in the refrigerator that is full of rotted food. You open the fridge and let your eyes wander across numerous containers, completely unaware of the rancid goods that are waiting to be discovered. While we are yet unaware of the impending rot hiding in the container, we have no concern for it. We rifle through the fridge as if all is well. Grabbing that one container and flipping the lid off, we instantly realize there is something not right and dispose of it. No one stands, looking at the mouldy leftovers, contemplating whether or not it should be disposed of—it's a no-brainer.

So it is with the rubbish in our own lives. While we are unaware, we walk through each day oblivious to the fact that we have unopened containers in our hearts that are housing rot and rubbish. If we wish to parent well and live a life of joy and complete freedom, we must take an inventory—even when it is hard—of the containers in our hearts. We must find where the rubbish is being contained and completely discard it immediately. One way of discovering the rotten containers is to ask God to reveal them. He will show us exactly what areas we need to look at and where our rubbish is being stored.

Let's take a look at some of the most common pieces of rubbish that single moms unknowingly allow to dictate their identity. Keep in mind that we are most often oblivious to the fact that these long buried beliefs have shaped much of how we relate to others—and to our children.

## Unforgiveness

Forgiveness is essential both for our own freedom and for the freedom of our children. Forgiving those who inflicted wounds does not mean that the hurtful treatment was okay or that we forget it. Forgiveness simply means we are choosing to release that other person from paying the penalty that we think they owe us, just like Christ did when He took our sin onto His own self and hung on the cross. Forgiveness is done for our own freedom, not the other person's. When we forgive, we are releasing ourselves from the control the other person's actions has held over us.

It is only when we absolutely forgive those who rejected us or bullied us or put the knife in our back that we can step out from behind the walls and love our children the way they deserve to be loved. It is only when we realize and believe who Christ says we are that we will be able to have reasonable boundaries and expectations for our children and parent them in a healthy, loving, and secure manner.

## Guilt

The weight of guilt is heavy and causes us to feel as though we have done wrong or have failed in some obligation. Guilt is difficult to explain; however, we have all experienced the sharpness of its sting. It can take on a whole empire of seemingly logical reasons. "My children are missing out on a father." "If I would have been thinner or sexier or just more attractive, my husband would not have left." "I'm a terrible mother... I'm always tired and never have the energy or patience to deal with the kids." "I yelled at my teenager this morning."

Sound familiar? Come on now, if you are a single mom, it's a given that you have had some of these thoughts—or others very similar—running through your mind on a somewhat regular basis. Good news, moms: the time has come to put down all that heavy, joy-robbing guilt.

Guilt serves no purpose other than to constantly remind us of our perceived failures. There is certainly no purpose in that, because we are not failures. We may fail from time to time—everyone does—but that does not make us failures any more than walking through the garage every now and then makes us a car.

The only way to find release from the heavy weight of guilt is to simply put it down. If your child was holding a bag full of rocks and, looking up at you in agony cried, "Mommy, this is too heavy for me," what would you tell him? "Put it down, you silly boy," is what I would say, and that is what the Lord is saying to all of us who are carrying the burdensome load of guilt.

Put it down ladies, and absolutely refuse to pick it up again. It is impossible to parent well when we are bent over and beat up under the weight of guilt. All of us will stumble and fall down—so get up, wipe the dirt off, and keep going. Step out of the guilt trap that has you ensnared and step into the freedom and blessing Christ is offering you.

## Condemnation

Condemnation is not the same as guilt; guilt is self-inflicted whereas condemnation is others-inflicted. Others seem to have the ability to cause us to feel bad, to feel like a failure, by making comments like "How could you let your children go with him?" or "Your kids must really miss their father." People can unintentionally be cruel. Often they believe they are helping by their comments, intending sympathy or concern.

Still other individuals do intentionally go out of their way to make us feel awful and they make their best efforts to heap all kinds of negative emotions squarely on our shoulders. Not too long ago, I received an anonymous email, although the person was not sneaky enough to avoid being caught. It was absolutely intended to make me feel pain by comments such as "If you haven't made it by the time you are forty, you never will... I won't be surprised when you are back living in a trailer in the middle of nowhere."

Now, my first reaction to such a horrible letter was, "What is wrong with living in a trailer?" My favourite home was the cozy little mobile home where I raised my three sons for a number of years. My second thought was, "I'm not forty yet, but your idea of 'making it' and mine are probably not the same." There were numerous other things that I won't mention here, but the person was so impudent as to require a police investigation, resulting in a legal no contact order.

This individual's intention was to weigh me down with condemnation and I could have easily succumbed to that, had it arrived five years prior. However, because I had already discovered my true identity in Christ, it had no effect on me other than to cause me to wonder why people can be so simple-minded as to think they have the answers to everyone's business.

Besides ignorant and oblivious individuals lavishing condemnation on us, the devil also likes to attack us with condemnation. I believe it is one of his favourite tools, because with it he can often throw us off track and cause us to doubt Christ's unconditional love and forgiveness.

Romans 8:1 reminds us that we are safe from such condemning weight. "There is now *no* condemnation for those who are Christ Jesus." It does not say "only a wee bit," or "when we really mess up," or even "if we have been wounded and scarred." Did you get that? It says *no* condemnation. None. Nada. Zilch. Zero. So hold your head up high, ladies, and boldly walk out from behind the shadows of condemnation. You are free— Jesus Christ Himself says so and that is someone we can absolutely, unequivocally, irrefutably believe.

## Rejection

Rejection feels like we are being dismissed because we fail to meet someone's standards. Rejection is very painful because it is very real. When we have been rejected, it hurts because it strips us of our value. The more times we feel rejected, the deeper the wound gets. When that rejection is by a spouse or someone we have trusted enough to give ourselves to, it cuts right to our soul. When we have a child and watch that child bear the pain of being rejected by their father, it hurts exponentially. We carry their rejection as well as our own and it's much too heavy for our lil ol' shoulders.

The opposite of rejection is acceptance. There is One who accepts us always—no matter what we have done or not done. That One is Christ. He unconditionally accepted us before we even knew Him. He accepts us when we are angry and when we are kicking and screaming and pitching a fit. There are no expectations we must meet or tests we must pass before He will accept us. He just does!

There are always consequences for our choices—good consequences for good choices and negative consequences for bad choices, but His acceptance *never* wavers or changes. There is nothing we can do to change how He feels about us—absolutely nothing.

Rejection hurts deeply, but it need not destroy us. It is absurd to think we can parent well while entangled in the invisible threads of rejection. We become so entangled that we lose our ability to trust. We absolutely must break free from those debilitating threads of rejection and step into the secure place where we are able to grasp tightly to the acceptance of Christ. Our security is not in people, but in Christ where no man shall ever take me out of His hands (John 10:28).

These are just a few scraps from the mound of rubbish that we may be living under without even knowing it. While unforgiveness, guilt, condemnation, and rejection may be some of the more common bits of trash, there are so many other bits and pieces that may be buried deep within ourselves.

I encourage you to spend some time and see which piles of rubbish you are still holding onto. We all want to be good parents and love our children in a way that will empower them to be sensational individuals in a harsh world. In order to accomplish such a task, we must put down our rubbish and determine to never pick it up again. Leave it at the cross and Jesus will happily dispose of it for you.

# A NEW YOU

Who are you? Sounds like a simple question, doesn't it? You probably answer such a question similarly to how everyone else would answer. When that question is asked, people usually start by giving their names. They give their title or position at the office or workplace—a receptionist, school teacher, manager, or CEO—or they give their title at home. We are mom or grandma or auntie or sister or daughter.

We might possibly continue on and give our address or our age. (We are all twenty-nine, aren't we?) We might even list our children giving their names and spewing off their little characteristics and quirks.

Fortunately, none of these things are who we are. All the things above describe particular aspects of us—our characteristics or connections—but they do not define who we are. There is a very good chance that we don't even know who we are. Most people don't. Single moms in particular have difficulty with their identity. We somehow get lost between the cracks of what was and what should have been.

When we have been hurt, rejected and broken, we attempt to avoid feeling the pain of those things. We hide behind masks. We put on smiling faces and act like everything is okay when we—and everyone around us—know differently. How can we positively parent our children when we are overburdened with past pains and current nightmares?

Hopefully, after reading the last chapter, you have made the crucial decision to say goodbye to all the rubbish you were carrying for so long. Once we put down that rubbish, we are left with empty hands that we often don't know what to do with. Once we have cleaned out our hearts and minds of the rubbish, we need to fill them with the good things God promises. Those good things begin by learning to wear the identity that comes with being a daughter of the most high God.

One of the keys to great parenting is the ability to consistently put down our rubbish and pick up the truth that Christ offers. Woven delicately but boldly throughout His Word is the truth of our identity—who we really are, not who we've believed ourselves to be or been told we are. It's relatively simple to find our identity in the "rubbish" that we carry around from the past, but that is a false identity.

Like someone putting on a mask and pretending to be someone else, so it is with the masks we put on and hide behind. Everyone might see us as the masks appear, but behind the mask is our true God-given identity—the one that will change our lives, our beliefs, and our parenting.

It's quite simple to be incompetent. It is easy to believe that we are exactly what our wounds tell us we are: losers, unable, ugly, broken, unworthy, unlovable, and rejected. Regardless of who the past may try to convince us we are, the Word of God says to *"forget the former things; do not dwell on the past"* (Isaiah 43:18).

We are to look to Him for a healthy, positive present and future, forgetting our past mistakes and burdens which have kept us bound for so long. It is time to step out of those heavy clanging chains that have had us bound and walk into the freedom of God's truth.

## But It's Not Fair

Commonly, when a woman finds herself raising kids alone, she understandably decides to fight for this and that through the

# A NEW YOU

Who are you? Sounds like a simple question, doesn't it? You probably answer such a question similarly to how everyone else would answer. When that question is asked, people usually start by giving their names. They give their title or position at the office or workplace—a receptionist, school teacher, manager, or CEO—or they give their title at home. We are mom or grandma or auntie or sister or daughter.

We might possibly continue on and give our address or our age. (We are all twenty-nine, aren't we?) We might even list our children giving their names and spewing off their little characteristics and quirks.

Fortunately, none of these things are who we are. All the things above describe particular aspects of us—our characteristics or connections—but they do not define who we are. There is a very good chance that we don't even know who we are. Most people don't. Single moms in particular have difficulty with their identity. We somehow get lost between the cracks of what was and what should have been.

When we have been hurt, rejected and broken, we attempt to avoid feeling the pain of those things. We hide behind masks. We put on smiling faces and act like everything is okay when we—and everyone around us—know differently. How can we positively parent our children when we are overburdened with past pains and current nightmares?

Hopefully, after reading the last chapter, you have made the crucial decision to say goodbye to all the rubbish you were courts, whether in mediation, in chambers, or with a judge ruling. Unfortunately, single moms often have a difficult time manoeuvring the legal system and its legal proceedings and rulings rarely turn out to be fair (at least from our perspective).

We certainly cannot always trust our Western social systems; judges and rulers have been tainted by their own circumstances, ethics, and beliefs. Perhaps they or their children have been through a nasty, painful divorce where one party put the other through a horrible public display. Let's face it. Our systems are not fair because life is not fair and that taints people's outlooks and beliefs.

Even in bible times, this was true. There is a story in Luke which starts out "in a certain town there was a judge who neither feared God nor cared about men [or women]" (Luke 18:2).

You may have faced horribly unfair circumstances in your life which others whom have not walked this path can only try to understand. I hear far too many stories where there is nothing but pain and regret—pain from other peoples choices and regret from our own. Life just seems unfair, and indeed it is. Remember the old saying, "all is fair in love and war?" That all is fair line actually means that anything goes, do whatever you must to win, fairness is irrelevant.

There have been countless times throughout my own mothering years, raising three sons alone, where I have slumped hopelessly into the overstuffed, worn-out, coffee-stained rocking chair and sobbed, "It's just not fair." I cry to the Lord. I yell and scream and throw quite the self-pitying temper tantrums. He patiently listens and waits.

When I finally become exhausted and am quiet long enough for the Lord's still small voice to be heard, He always tells me the same thing. He says, "Daughter, I never promised life to be fair, but I did promise to love you and give you peace when the unfairness of life gets too heavy. Rest in me."

Unfortunately, there is nothing in life that's fair. However, if we can learn to trust in the Lord, it is much easier to let go of our demands for "fairness" and simply trust that He is in control of our circumstances and knows exactly what He's doing. No matter how unfair we believe our situation to be, our Father will always be with us, no matter what storm we may stumble through on our journey.

*"Now there is in store for me a crown of righteousness, which the Lord, the righteous Judge, will award to me on that day"* (2 Timothy 4:8). There is a judge who is righteous and He will ensure that we are given back everything that has been taken from us. He will emphatically make all the wrongs right. He will undoubtedly bring His own fairness to our situations.

### Make a Trade

What if you found a store where you could trade in your old dilapidated junk for brand new items? Wouldn't you gladly give up that old, smelly, on-its-last-legs sofa in exchange for a brand new comfortable Lagona microfibre sleeper sofa? How about the rickety kitchen table and chairs set that came from old Uncle Dan's farm auction which should have been thrown into the burn pile but now sits in your kitchen?

Wouldn't you be amazed if you could drag it to the store and the store owner would take it in an even trade for the best, solid oak table and queen style chairs? I don't know anyone who would say, "No thanks. I'll just hold onto my old rubbish and continue to pour on the super glue or wrap on another layer of duct tape and pray it doesn't fall apart."

That would be completely crazy. If there were such a store (and there isn't, so don't go looking) that would be the busiest store on the planet. Everyone would know about it. People from far and wide would drag their old junk to this trade-in shop. There

You see, you are not who your circumstances say you are. You are not worth what the loans officer harassing you makes you feel like you are worth. You are not what the nosey old ninny down the street says you are and you are not who the group of young marrieds in the middle section of church believe you to be.

I speak from experience. Picture this—a small seemingly naive blonde lady, looking weary and ragged, shows up to church. Over one arm is draped an overstuffed bag with an over worn teddy bear peeking out of the top and in the other arm a sleeping four-year-old boy. Lagging somewhere close behind are two other boys, most likely groaning about having to be in church.

As this frazzled lady is looking desperately for a seat big enough for her little crew, you see people start to shuffle in their seats. They are not shuffling closer together to make room for her, but rather they are spreading apart, setting their jackets or bags on the seat beside them, just to ensure there is no room for her crew to sit.

Finally, she spots a row very close to the front and after gently prodding her two boys into the seat, lays the sleeping one down on the bench. Again you can see people moving away, not wanting to get too close, just in case these boys start to get out of control and this little mom can't reel them in.

Everyone has an opinion and while some are silly enough to verbalize it, others just show it in their pitiful glances and judgmental stares, but at the end of the day, it is only the truth of God's word that matters. The truth is that you are bought with the blood of a King. God knew exactly what He was doing when He created you. God approves of you. He knew you long before the foundation of the world was set in place. He loved you from the very beginning. In fact, He adored you before there was a beginning.

Let your mind wander for a brief moment. Before God created the heavens or the earth, before He instructed the water to part or

would be no need for million dollar advertising budge
word of mouth would be faster and much more produ
lines would be lengthy, but we would happily stan
endless lines for however long it took to get a turn in su

This may be nothing more than my very own litt
store, but there is something far greater which is a rea
about your own life? Something far more valuable then
kitchen set is at stake here. It's you and me. Would
unimaginable if we could take our lives the way they are
up, damaged, worn out, scared, and misused—and trade
for something brand new? A life that is whole and con
peace and full of joy? Good news, ladies—you can do
Doesn't seem fair, does it?

It is a good thing, really, that life is not fair. If it were, w
be unable to trade in our old worn-out, broken, worthles
for the new, pure, and spotless selves that God is freely
us.

I have had some fairly tough experiences in this strang
we call life and I bet you have, too. I have visible scars to
me, but the invisible wounds have been healed.

When the world says you are "just a single mom" withou
and running on the wheel of never-ending failure and d
God says you are chosen, holy and dearly loved. When th
says you are in debt and are dragging the ball and chain of po
God says that He supplies all your needs and that if yc
faithful, you will be richly blessed. When people look at you
that sadness of pity and you feel pitiful, God says that you
need to worry about anything, but by praying with thankfu
He will wrap you in His peace and protect your heart and n

It all comes down to a personal choice. Who are you goii
believe? The ones who are judging you because of unde
circumstances, or the One who created you in His very
image? Those who only cast you pity or the One who says you
worthy to be called His precious daughter in whom He deligl

the stars to shine, He had you in mind. I wonder sometimes, if He had to create the world just so that you and I had a magnificent place to dwell.

It reminds me of a woman who finds out she is going to have a baby. This mom spends weeks preparing the baby's room. She carefully decides on a paint pallet and painstakingly scatters rainbows and butterflies over the freshly painted walls. She rubs her growing belly and goes shopping to find the perfect crib set and blankets. After all, one of these blankets may very well end up being "thee blankey," which the child drags around for years to come.

Are you getting my drift? We go to ridiculous lengths to set up and prepare the perfect space for our upcoming bundle of joy who, by the way, will never fully appreciate all we did to prepare their space.

That is a tiny little glimmer at what God did for you and I. He knew we were coming because He had already planned for us— He already knew us intimately. Because He had already planned for us, He had to create a space for us to dwell. He did a magnificent job with His creative paint pallet of vivid blue skies and green grass, juicy red, orange, and yellow fruit hanging from a medley of trees. He called it the earth. He did that just for you and me, His children.

God has a uniquely special plan in mind and now it is up to you to move towards that destiny. While we might face difficult circumstances, God will never say, "Well, you are now a big fat failure and I'm just going to give up on you and choose someone much more deserving to take your place and fulfill the destiny I planned for you." He never says we blew it. He never says we failed. He never says goodbye.

God made you with a purpose and a destiny in mind and no other individual He created can fulfill it—it fits only you. Like the glass slipper, God's purposes are not a "one size fits all."

Colossians 3:12 tells us that we are *"God's chosen people, holy and dearly loved."* God chose us because He knows us. He knows that we have value and purpose. He created us to be just like Him and He allows opportunities for us to become like Him.

God created us in such a way as to experience His goodness. We cannot know what peace is unless we experience unrest. It is impossible to enjoy God's joy when we've never been touched by life's sorrows. None of us would recognize God's acceptance if we didn't first feel the sting or rejection. We could not possibly understand God's grace if we didn't realize our need for His pardon.

*"Listen, O daughter, consider and give ear...the King is enthralled by your beauty; honor him, for he is your Lord"* (Psalm 45:10-11).

We are aware that God catches every one of our tears and puts them in a jar. When you are in the middle of a breakdown, doubled over with pain and tears that simply will not shut off, picture God. He literally pulls you towards Himself and holds you while you hurt. He comforts you and says it was "for those tears" that He died.

*"The Lord your God is with you, he is mighty to save. He will take great delight in you, he will quiet you with his love, and he will rejoice over you with singing"* (Zephaniah 3:17).

He delights in you, mom, and when you are hurting or broken, He covers you and sings over you. Imagine that. When our own children are sick or have been hurt, we pick them up and snuggle them close to us. We may not know what to say or have any answers for them to soften their hurts, but our mere presence and touch speaks louder than any words we could say. When we wipe their little tears with our sleeve, they feel comfort and somehow it causes the pain to hurt just a little bit less.

That is what God does with us. We are His pride and joy. When our Father sees us hurting and wounded, He wants to take our

Colossians 3:12 tells us that we are *"God's chosen people, holy and dearly loved."* God chose us because He knows us. He knows that we have value and purpose. He created us to be just like Him and He allows opportunities for us to become like Him.

God created us in such a way as to experience His goodness. We cannot know what peace is unless we experience unrest. It is impossible to enjoy God's joy when we've never been touched by life's sorrows. None of us would recognize God's acceptance if we didn't first feel the sting or rejection. We could not possibly understand God's grace if we didn't realize our need for His pardon.

*"Listen, O daughter, consider and give ear...the King is enthralled by your beauty; honor him, for he is your Lord"* (Psalm 45:10-11).

We are aware that God catches every one of our tears and puts them in a jar. When you are in the middle of a breakdown, doubled over with pain and tears that simply will not shut off, picture God. He literally pulls you towards Himself and holds you while you hurt. He comforts you and says it was "for those tears" that He died.

*"The Lord your God is with you, he is mighty to save. He will take great delight in you, he will quiet you with his love, and he will rejoice over you with singing"* (Zephaniah 3:17).

He delights in you, mom, and when you are hurting or broken, He covers you and sings over you. Imagine that. When our own children are sick or have been hurt, we pick them up and snuggle them close to us. We may not know what to say or have any answers for them to soften their hurts, but our mere presence and touch speaks louder than any words we could say. When we wipe their little tears with our sleeve, they feel comfort and somehow it causes the pain to hurt just a little bit less.

That is what God does with us. We are His pride and joy. When our Father sees us hurting and wounded, He wants to take our the stars to shine, He had you in mind. I wonder sometimes, if He had to create the world just so that you and I had a magnificent place to dwell.

It reminds me of a woman who finds out she is going to have a baby. This mom spends weeks preparing the baby's room. She carefully decides on a paint pallet and painstakingly scatters rainbows and butterflies over the freshly painted walls. She rubs her growing belly and goes shopping to find the perfect crib set and blankets. After all, one of these blankets may very well end up being "thee blankey," which the child drags around for years to come.

Are you getting my drift? We go to ridiculous lengths to set up and prepare the perfect space for our upcoming bundle of joy who, by the way, will never fully appreciate all we did to prepare their space.

That is a tiny little glimmer at what God did for you and I. He knew we were coming because He had already planned for us— He already knew us intimately. Because He had already planned for us, He had to create a space for us to dwell. He did a magnificent job with His creative paint pallet of vivid blue skies and green grass, juicy red, orange, and yellow fruit hanging from a medley of trees. He called it the earth. He did that just for you and me, His children.

God has a uniquely special plan in mind and now it is up to you to move towards that destiny. While we might face difficult circumstances, God will never say, "Well, you are now a big fat failure and I'm just going to give up on you and choose someone much more deserving to take your place and fulfill the destiny I planned for you." He never says we blew it. He never says we failed. He never says goodbye.

God made you with a purpose and a destiny in mind and no other individual He created can fulfill it—it fits only you. Like the glass slipper, God's purposes are not a "one size fits all."

would be no need for million dollar advertising budgets because word of mouth would be faster and much more productive. The lines would be lengthy, but we would happily stand in those endless lines for however long it took to get a turn in such a shop.

This may be nothing more than my very own little fantasy store, but there is something far greater which is a reality. How about your own life? Something far more valuable then a sofa or kitchen set is at stake here. It's you and me. Wouldn't it be unimaginable if we could take our lives the way they are—busted up, damaged, worn out, scared, and misused—and trade them in for something brand new? A life that is whole and complete, at peace and full of joy? Good news, ladies—you can do just that.

Doesn't it seem fair, does it?

It is a good thing, really, that life is not fair. If it were, we would be unable to trade in our old worn-out, broken, worthless selves for the new, pure, and spotless selves that God is freely offering us.

I have had some fairly tough experiences in this strange thing we call life and I bet you have, too. I have visible scars to remind me, but the invisible wounds have been healed.

When the world says you are "just a single mom" without hope and running on the wheel of never-ending failure and despair. God says you are chosen, holy and dearly loved. When the bank says you are in debt and are dragging the ball and chain of poverty, God says that He supplies all your needs and that if you are faithful, you will be richly blessed. When people look at you with that sadness of pity and you feel pitiful, God says that you don't need to worry about anything, but by praying with thankfulness He will wrap you in His peace and protect your heart and mind. It all comes down to a personal choice. Who are you going to believe? The ones who are judging you because of undesired circumstances, or the One who created you in His very own image? Those who only cast you pity or the One who says you are worthy to be called His precious daughter in whom He delights?

You see, you are not who your circumstances say you are. You are not worth what the loans officer harassing you makes you feel like you are worth. You are not what the nosey old ninny down the street says you are and you are not who the group of young marrieds in the middle section of church believe you to be.

I speak from experience. Picture this—a small seemingly naïve blonde lady, looking weary and ragged, shows up to church. Over one arm is draped an overstuffed bag with an over worn teddy bear peeking out of the top and in the other arm a sleeping four-year-old boy. Lagging somewhere close behind are two other boys, most likely groaning about having to be in church. As this frazzled lady is looking desperately for a seat big enough for her little crew, you see people start to shuffle in their seats. They are not shuffling closer together to make room for her, but rather they are spreading apart, setting their jackets or bags on the seat beside them, just to ensure there is no room for her crew to sit.

Finally, she spots a row very close to the front and after gently prodding her two boys into the seat, lays the sleeping one down on the bench. Again you can see people moving away, not wanting to get too close, just in case these boys start to get out of control and this little mom can't reel them in.

Everyone has an opinion and while some are silly enough to verbalize it, others just show it in their pitiful glances and judgmental stares, but at the end of the day, it is only the truth of God's word that matters. The truth is that you are bought with the blood of a King. God knew exactly what He was doing when He created you. God approves of you. He knew you long before the foundation of the world was set in place. He loved you from the very beginning. In fact, He adored you before there was a beginning.

Let your mind wander for a brief moment. Before God created the heavens or the earth, before He instructed the water to part or heaviness in trade for praise, our chains in trade for freedom, and our brokenness in trade for peace. *"He is a rewarder of those who diligently seek Him"* (Hebrews 11:6, NKJV). If you wait on the Lord, He will strengthen you and He will heal up your wounds. Our Heavenly Father will lift you up and break the chains that hold you. God will loose the bands from around your neck and He will give you the garment of praise for the spirit of heaviness (Isaiah 61:3).

None of that is a fair trade, but it is all in our favour. It is not fair that God sent His only son to the death of the cross so that you and I could exchange our death for His life. Thank God that life is not fair.

## I Am What I Am

You are God's seed of heaven. You have the blood of the Holy One flowing through your veins. You are the daughter with whom Jesus Christ is well pleased and there is nothing you can do to be anything less. However, you must choose to walk in it.

It is high time you put on the robe of righteousness which God has been trying to clothe you with. His Son died so that you could be clean and holy, but it is up to you to start walking in that truth.

The Word of God says that you have a purpose. God put you on the earth at this precise moment, knowing the circumstances in which you would find yourself. He knew that you would be a single mom, and guess what? He knew that you would do an excellent job of raising up his children. He trusted you with those little babies whom He absolutely adores because He knew that you were trustworthy to look after them well.

You were not created to be a nobody. You certainly were not created to be average. You were created with purpose and Christ has filled you with everything you need to fulfill that purpose.

41

Now, I can hear you saying, "Yeah sure, maybe you, but certainly not me." Listen up, ladies: just because we may not believe something does not make it untrue. Truth is truth regardless who does or does not believe it. It's up to you. Adorn yourself in the truth, begin walking in the truth, and just as God has promised, the truth will indeed set you free.

Jeremiah 29:11 says, "'*For I know the plans I have for you*' *declares the LORD, 'plans to prosper you and not to harm you, plans to give you hope and a future.*'" Does that sound like you were put here for a purpose? It certainly doesn't sound like you are here by happenstance.

God Himself says that you are valuable. He has you in the palm of His hand and is just waiting for you to ask Him to take control of your life and lead you into the plans and purposes that He has for you. You will be amazed at what He has in store just for you and your children.

The Word says that the Lord has ordered your steps, but you must want to walk in those steps.

Think about that for just a moment. When my sons were little, I took them on a little sightseeing adventure. I drove to this little secluded spot that I used to visit when I was a girl. Behind the bushes and trees were a number of enormous sand dunes and walking paths. My little boys spent hours sliding down the sand and climbing back up again, giggling and having all sorts of fun.

Just a few feet from the mountainous sandy path, a climbing path had been carved out of rock. If you have ever tried to climb up a steep mountain of fine sand, you will know how difficult— nearly impossible—that climb can be. You get a few feet up and then all of a sudden slide right back down. It is exhausting and frustrating.

After watching the boys struggle to repeatedly climb up the slippery sand, I suggested they use the stone steps. They struggled and fell getting sand in their shoes and socks and underwear and hair and up their noses and between their toes, but they refused to use the steps. Eventually, once they were exhausted and so dirty I thought they might never come clean, they decided to use the stone steps and to their surprise, they were able to get to the top of the sand dunes without much effort whatsoever.

This is how we tend to function. God has ordered our steps— that means He's laid them out for us, but if we refuse to walk on them, our journey is long and hard and dirty. We get bruised and beat up. It is not until we are worn out and exhausted that we fall down before Him, give in, and use the steps He has laid out for us.

Today's the day. Begin believing the truth about yourself. Start speaking it. Begin walking in it. Peel off the negative thoughts and images you have been walking in and put on the truth of God's Word.

You are forever secure in His presence because He will never leave you. He adores you and wants you to rise up to His purposes. There is absolutely nothing you can do to decrease His love for you and there is certainly nothing you can do to increase His love for you. God loves you because of who God is, not because of who you are. He created you with all your quirks and eccentricities for *his* benefit, not yours.

He did not create you to be less than. He did not create you to be adequate or even average. He created you to be spectacular and purposeful and valuable. So rise up and allow God to lead you into all the amazing things that He has planned just for you.

# Section Two—Valuing My Children

Psalm 127:3—*Sons [daughters] are a heritage from the Lord, children a reward from him.*

There is no greater gift than your children. You may not believe they are a gift on those exhausting days when you are lonely and trying desperately to be both mom and dad. You may not see them as valuable after they take their frustration out on you because you are the one there for them. You might be looking for a return policy.

Stop looking and start enjoying. Life is short, so enjoy what you have. You may be angry and frustrated and broken but you have the biggest blessings in the world looking up at you—your children. Start to value those little gifts called children and when you do, your whole world just might change for the better and the Son will begin to shine once again.

# TAME YOUR TONGUE

*He who guards his lips guards his life, but he who speaks rashly will come to ruin.* Proverbs 13:3

"Sticks and stones may break my bones but words will never hurt me." Such a silly old saying, really. I remember my mother teaching it to me in elementary school when Gary Thompson, one of the grade four boys, had an enormous crush on me and was being childishly mean. You remember grade four, don't you? When little Johnny is crushing on little Mary? Mary is destined to get an eraser thrown at her, smacked by a ruler, or—even worse—pushed into the garbage bins during morning recess.

Well, Gary didn't have a crush on me for long and by the time we hit fifth grade, he had moved on to throwing chalk at Wendy McGilly. About the second day of fifth grade, Wendy McGilly punched Gary Thompson square in the face, causing his nose to bleed all over his desk. From that day on, of course, Gary Thompson was absolutely certain that Wendy McGilly would love him forever. She didn't.

We all got through the elementary years nearly unscathed (I ended up with only one scar in the middle of my forehead, but that was not from Gary Thompson). I have had all my sons go through elementary school and one by one they each hit fourth grade. Sure enough, during their grade four year each one of them came home agitated that one of the little girls had said they were funny looking or thrown a rock or stabbed them with a pencil or wiped something disgusting on their jackets.

Like any other mother who doesn't know what to say to such a predicament and is trying with all the willpower she can muster to stifle any appearance of a giggle, I would sing the little ditty and inform them that it was merely a crush and they would survive it just like the millions of fourth graders before them and the millions of fourth graders to follow.

Today, however, I sing a different tune, and so should every mother. In fact, "Sticks and stones may break my bones but words will never hurt me" is actually a big fat lie. Just because we stuck the silly words within chords of a catchy little tune does not make it true—or cute. It is a lie that we unknowingly teach our children.

Certainly, sticks and stones may break my bones but bones, contusions, scrapes and bruises heal, usually without leaving a scar. But words? Words are deadly. Words can cut to the very core of our being, shredding our hearts and twisting our minds. Words can damage us irreparably and if we are not very careful, our own words can damage our precious children to the point of no return. Once harsh words have left our mouths, they will find their target and land, injecting their deadly poison.

I know this for absolutely certain because of a number of friends whom have been in some very abusive relationships. They have been smacked, punched, pushed, and thrown around. They have also been verbally attacked. There is an interesting similarity between all these women; every single one of them, without exception, say they would far rather be physically attacked then mentally or verbally attacked.

Their reasoning? Their physical injuries heal and their attackers usually apologize and are, at least for a little while, filled with remorse. Of course, there are exceptions to this rule, but for the most part people feel apologetic when they leave a bruise or a broken bone or a scar on someone they are supposed to love. Somehow, it seems more wrong if there is a visible mark left which can be seen.

The injuries left by the attack of demeaning and hurtful words often do not heal but rather leave very painful scars. Those who attack with their words are often unaware they are doing anything wrong so rarely do they apologize or feel remorse of any type. Rather, they claim the person who was their target is "too sensitive," or "blows things out of proportion," making the damage that much worse.

Mean and hateful words cause one to wonder what is wrong with them. Are they really as insignificant and stupid as their attacker implies?

The Word of God is so clear on words and our tongue that we absolutely must pay attention. Words have the power to give life or the power to destroy life. Proverbs 25:11 says "a word aptly spoken is like apples of gold in settings of silver."

Matthew 12:36-37 reminds us again about the power of our words in the life beyond this world. "But I tell you that men will have to give account on the day of judgment for every careless word they have spoken. For by your words you will be acquitted and by your words you will be condemned."

It is said that words can either bring life or death. Proverbs 18:21 says, "The tongue has the power of life and death." If you have ever been on the receiving end of a verbal assault, you will understand the harsh truth of that saying. It can literally kill your spirit.

Likewise, our own words can bring our children life or it can bring them death. It may not be a physical death, but the death of one's self-worth is excruciatingly painful and very difficult to recover from, especially when those words come from someone we love and trust.

Turn your eyes for just a moment to your children. Have you said things that should not have been said? We can tell someone they are stupid without ever saying the words, "You're stupid." We can naively imply meaning. For example, to say to your child,

"Why can't you get it? Will you ever learn? What is wrong with you?" Nowhere in those few common statements was the word "stupid," but it was certainly implied.

There are numerous areas where we need to watch our mouths. Let's journey through a few of the traps where we often unconsciously speak or imply negative hurtful words so that we are better able to make a conscious choice to speak life to our children.

## Don't Dishonour Dad

*"Do not repay anyone evil with evil. Be careful to do what is right in the eyes of everybody"* (Romans 12:17).

Divorced people are famous for their mud flinging skills. Incidentally, mud flinging can occur whether or not there was ever a legally binding marriage ceremony. Referring to your child's father as a "sperm donor" or "the ghost man" is very painful and damaging to your child. Remember, children absolutely love their parents, both of them. They should *never* be made to feel that they cannot love one of you just as much as the other.

No child should ever need to pretend to one parent that they don't care about the other parent. Deep down, every child wants a relationship with both their parents. If you have one of those children who says otherwise, they are not being honest. They may have convinced themselves of this, but it is a tragic self-defence mechanism used to avoid rejection—a wall they have put up and a lie they have told themselves long enough to believe. The truth, however, is that they will always deeply desire a relationship with both their parents.

Truth be told, all we single moms could easily get together and sit down over an intravenous drip of hot, jacked-up coffee and spend hours comparing horror stories of our children's fathers. We could each outdo the other and despair over who had it the worst. The daddies are either non-existent or we wish they were. However, it is crucial to our children's well being (no matter how old they are) to realize that these stories are always viewed under the microscope of our own internalized pain, anger, and self-defence. It is always in our children's best interest to learn to bite our tongues and genuinely smile. Kids can spot a fake quite easily. Our kids should never hear our stories, because they are our stories, our points of view, our hurts, and our perspectives— not theirs.

*"The wise woman builds her house, but with her own hands [or mouth] the foolish one tears hers down"* (Proverbs 14:1). Memorize this verse, write it on your mirror, etch it into the deepest part of your heart and refer to it often.

The same scene from above could easily be set just a bit differently. Rather than a hundred women and an intravenous drip, insert a hundred men and a garage full of old cars and oily tools. You could change the beverage and the place of conversation but the stories would be the same. You know why? Because daddies are viewing their stories through the same glasses of pain, anger, and self-defence that us women are glaring through.

Granted, there are difficult circumstances when you are required to say something or give an explanation to your kids. Daddy might not show up for a visit or he may ditch them for a variety of reasons. Even still, be very careful what words come out of your mouth. If you are angry, take a few moments alone locked in your bathroom or bedroom and fall to your knees and ask God for wisdom. Always guard your tongue. Even when it hurts.

Sometimes kids need answers or explanations, but they do not need to hear our "take" and the answers need not be tainted with our opinions. Kids are very smart. They read us very well. We must learn to control not only our tongues, but also our eyes, our arms, our sighs, and all other possible body language. We can say the right words, but if we are huffing and rolling our eyes, kids will see right through it.

The truth is that everyone thinks they got the rotten end of the deal, and perhaps some of you did. To you it's an insurmountable problem but to your kids it is just mom and dad. They don't want to hear who did what to whom and why so and so said such and such. If they do want particular information, let them grow up so they can comprehend the answers to their questions. When they are much, much older you can share some of your experiences with them, but that's a different chapter—perhaps an entirely different book.

Often, when our children are acting out some annoying behaviour, such as being bossy, us moms will become frustrated and sometimes blurt out the dreaded words, "You are just like your father." *Never* say that in a negative manner, moms—it is exceptionally damaging to our little ones. They know that we are not exactly fond of their fathers (usually), so to spew out such a line tells them that we don't like them, either. Even if that is not what we mean, that is what they will hear.

Rather, find some things that their father is great at (come on now, moms, burry your pride and come up with something) and point that out. "You are just like your father," in this positive sense, will not only empower your children to love their father, but you will also make it okay for the kids to be who they are. They cannot change their DNA, so for us to tell them that we disapprove of half of it is death to them. Instead, bring life to our little ones by encouraging them in the positive genes they received from their father.

The Lord promises in Matthew 5:9, *"Blessed are the peacemakers for they will be called [daughters] of God."*

Regardless of the unfavourable circumstances you might find yourself in, when we become peacemakers and learn to shut our mouths and open our hearts, *"He will fill your mouths with laughter and your lips with shouts of joy"* (Job 8:21). Wouldn't you rather give the gift of laughter and joy to your children? You have the power to do so; the choice is yours.

As difficult as it might be, learn to be a cheerleader for your children's relationship with their father. Be positive. Think of something that he does well and make those comments to your children instead of the things he failed at. It is not for his benefit, or yours. It is for the emotional stability of your children. With that in mind, you *will* be able to do it. Furthermore, as an extra bonus, your children will deeply respect you for being positive and supportive of them in their relationship with their father.

## Cut Off the Critical Tongue

Kids (and all human beings for that matter) will always do something, say something, or act a certain way which we can criticize. If we look hard enough, we will certainly be able to find a plethora of items that we feel require our critical opinion. Now, I know us moms need to correct and discipline, but that does not mean criticize. There is an enormous difference between criticizing and correcting. Let's take a look…

Correction suggests that one must make a change in order to amend or resolve something, and while correction has the potential to bring pain or frustration in the moment, it should lead to a positive healthy outcome. Everyone needs correction.

When my brother, aged thirty-nine, decides to speed down the highway in his bright yellow Ford truck, and he sees the flashing red and blue lights in his rear-view mirror, he is about to get some correction. The police officer who writes him a ticket, which he must pay, is correcting him. The goal of the police officer is to have my brother not repeat the action of racing down the roads at ridiculously high speeds. The consequence of his wrong behaviour is a large sum of his hard-earned money.

It may or may not work. However, after numerous tickets, numerous withdrawals from the bank account to pay for the tickets, and a few well spoken words from his beautiful but brilliant wife, the chances are very good that he will slow down. Thus, the goal has been accomplished through correction. Now, three years after all the tickets have been paid for, my brother is not likely to spend much time thinking about the incidents. He may tell the story of the ticket-writing police officer a few times, but his self-worth, mental-state and emotional well-being will not have been jeopardized.

Similarly, we correct our children for the long-term outcome. We do this in such a way as to direct them to positive action without damaging their mental or emotional states or put a nick in their personal self-worth or value.

On the other hand, criticism points out or magnifies the faults of someone in a way that brings emotional hurt. This is both destructive and damaging and will lead to negative and harmful behaviour and attitudes in both the one giving and the one receiving the criticism.

Criticism involves damaging words such as "You're bad," or "You look like a tramp" or "Are you retarded?" A verbal attack does not bring correction. It does bring heartbreak and pain. It does cause the recipient to feel devalued, unimportant, rejected, and hurt. It causes one to wonder what good they are. This is not what we want to do to our children.

In other chapters, we will look at what is 'correctable behaviour,' but here we are making a distinction between correcting, which is positive, and criticizing, which is negative. One brings life, the other brings death. Moms, be conscious of your words, and think before you speak. It's a matter of life and death.

Recently, I had an individual come to me and ask if I would be willing to talk to her son. He was acting angry and aggressive towards his parents and they had no idea why. His friends were the same friends he'd always had, his grades were not dropping and it appeared that he was his old happy self everywhere but at home.

This charming young man and I went for a coffee one evening and we talked. He opened up about his friends, girls, his sisters, and everything that concerned him—except for his parents. When I asked why he skipped over the most influential people in his life, he just looked at me blankly and said, "Why would I want to talk about them? They don't even like me."

Surprised by his statement, I asked what made him think this. It all stemmed from one comment made by his father a few weeks prior to his mood change. His father had angrily blurted out to this young man, "I really do not like who you are right now."

This young man went on to say that his parents did not like his hairstyle because it was scruffy. They did not like this, that, and the other thing about him and because of these little comments over the past number of weeks, this boy had internalized a belief that his parents simply did not like him and did not want him around.

In this young man's mind, if his own parents did not like him, he must be unlikable and thus, unlovable. His self-worth had spiralled and crashed. His spirit was wounded.

Speaking to his parents later, they of course were horrified. They are a wonderful Christian family who very much adore their children and deeply love the Lord. Unfortunately, when they became frustrated with their son, instead of using positive words and relating acceptance and unconditional love, they let their mouths get the best of them and unintentionally spewed hurtful, damaging words.

It is so easy to do. We don't regularly think before we speak. Words cannot be gathered and returned to the mouth they escaped from. Words cannot be unheard once they are heard. It's like toothpaste. With one big squeeze, you can make an enormous mess, but once you squeeze the toothpaste out of the tube, there is no way you can get it back in. The mess has been made. You can try with all your might to clean it up, but the mess has been made, the damage has been done.

Words contain power. Often a sincere apology can bring peace to a tumultuous situation. The power of encouraging words can actually transform a life. Speak the Word of God over your children regularly.

When your children are feeling angry or sad about the loss of their father, you don't need to have all the answers. Often, simply saying that while you cannot understand the depth of their pain, you want your child to know that you are there to listen without judgement for as long as the child needs. Reaffirm your love for the child and then just listen. Be careful not to say you understand, if in fact you do not. This can cause your child to be resentful and can quickly turn into being about you rather than being about them.

Sadly, there will be times when your child is angry at their father and needs a safe place to share their negative feelings, anger and sadness. You want to be that safe place for them, so you must learn to listen empathetically and sincerely without adding your negative comments.

When little Andrew cries through clenched teeth, "I hate him—I just hate him. He never does what he says he's going to do," do not join in on Andrew's outburst and put in your own comments. The most loving, beneficial way a mom can handle such a painful situation is to lovingly touch Andrew's arm or put her arm around his shoulder and calmly offer empathy. You need not stick up for or defend their father, but a genuine comment such as, "Andrew, I am so sorry you are hurt and angry right now. I want you to know that you are deeply cherished and valuable. I am so proud of what an excellent young man you are becoming," can make all the difference in the world, both to Andrew and to your relationship with him.

It is words of empathy and love that will enable Andrew, or your own children, to feel the pain and anger, but be able to put it down and move past it. These are all necessary tools our children need to become healthy individuals.

## Engage in Encouragement

Encouragement brings support, confidence, or hope to someone who is having a difficult time.

Encouragement is a key to unlocking your child's potential. Encouragement is easy in theory, although we often find it difficult to execute. Encouragement is simply opening our mouths and speaking out the positive things that are in our heart.

When we get into a habit of always speaking the negative "That colour doesn't really suit you," "Your hair looks terrible like that," "You have way too much make-up on," it can often be very difficult to get out of that habit and start speaking encouragement. Encouragement is just the opposite of criticism. They have no equal value, nor do they balance each other out. It takes a hundred bits of encouragement to erase the one critical word.

When we want to impart encouragement to our children, we can do so in passing and they will hear us. However, if we want them to really hear us and to feel the full effect of such encouragement, stop, take their hands, and look them straight in the eye as you say genuine words of encouragement.

As mothers, we must operate in encouragement with our children. Just because we feel okay does not mean they feel okay, and often a pat on the shoulder or a simple hug done in love will bring waves of encouragement. You can text them a quick word of encouragement when they are out with friends, or take some time and write them a heartfelt, well thought out note or email encouraging them in their day during a difficult time, or for no reason at all. Take the time to encourage your children and watch them blossom.

Words have exponentially powerful ramifications to motivate and change peoples lives.

The Word of God tells us to encourage one another and stay out of strife, to encourage one another and stir each other up to good works. According to Proverbs 18:21, death and life are in the power of the tongue. We can speak life or death to ourselves and to others, as well to the future. We can build up or tear down. We can encourage or discourage. When we speak good things into our children, good things will come out of our children.

When we do mess up and thoughtlessly spew out negative words, or come across to our children in a harsh manner with inappropriate tones and damaging words, it is absolutely necessary to immediately go to that child and apologize. It is amazing how children will learn to admire and respect you when you admit fault, take responsibility, and quickly apologize.

As a further benefit, when you apologize for your failures, you are modeling for them the very necessary life skill of taking personal responsibility and dealing with their actions appropriately. It is not in the being wrong where there is defeat, but in the inability to admit that wrong.

*"Let the words of my mouth and the meditation of my heart be acceptable in your sight"* (Psalms 19:14, NKJV). We cannot expect to speak healthy, positive, and encouraging words from our mouth if the thoughts in our heart are negative, cynical, or unfavourable. The words of our mouth will always follow the thoughts of our hearts. When we think positive thoughts about our children, positive words will come out of our mouths about our children, for *"out of the overflow of the heart, the mouth speaks"* (Matthew 12:34).

Now, that is not to say that we never take an opportunity to teach. If it is becoming too much of a problem, then you certainly need to pick out three or four reasonable outfits and let him choose between them. By doing so, you are having some control while still allowing your child to have some choices. You both win a battle that was never fought.

Please don't misunderstand this and think that I am saying teenagers should be able to wear whatever they choose—they need serious boundaries in their older years. As our kids get older, us moms can encourage appropriate clothing styles—after all, it is us who slides that little piece of hard plastic through the machine and pray to God it doesn't ring a bell and scream "declined."

Let's be reasonable here. Our teenagers cannot wear what we won't buy them. We do get to have some say in such matters, but we must be absolutely sure that we are instilling appropriateness rather than our own personal styles. Teaching appropriateness and purity starts in the preschool years and must be introduced there. Once the teenage years are in full swing, we must reinforce what we have already taught them each and every time they attempt to push the limits or test the boundaries.

We cannot have our little girls wearing tiny little skirts with their bottoms hanging out and then expect that when they are thirteen and fourteen they will suddenly have an inner knowledge of appropriateness. Furthermore, we absolutely must teach by example. We cannot expect our daughters to wear tops that cover their chests if we are walking around with cleavage to our belly buttons (quite honestly, after we've had a few children, everything eventually ends up around our belly button). It is up to us moms to model modesty and appropriateness in clothing. These are the things that we must be ready to battle if the time presents itself. Modesty and appropriateness is a battle worth fighting for.

Life is hard. There is no end to the negative things we can choose to dwell on. Similarly, there is also no end to the positive things we can dwell on. The problem is that it is much easier to see the negative and to wallow in it. It is a pattern-a habit that we get into, whether it is learned behaviour that we are unaware of or we have just had a tough road and are in the habit of expecting bad things. The choice is yours—make it wisely. Remember, "*a wise woman builds her house.*"

There is good news, ladies—you can choose to step from the darkness of negativity into the light of positivity.

So it's simple. Choose to guard your thoughts carefully, because what you think on, you will speak on. We need to learn to control our minds, for it is there that the battles are won or lost. What comes out of our mouths is simply a by-product of what is living in our heads.

Words…

Choose them wisely. When there are no good, positive words to say, say nothing.

*"He who guards his lips guards his life, but he who speaks rashly will come to ruin."* (Proverbs 13:3)

# BOUNDARIES & BATTLES

This chapter and the following one, "Consider Consistency," go hand in hand. Deciding which behaviours are worth battling for and which ones should be quietly overlooked is the initial step. The equally important secondary step is implementing your decisions with absolute consistency. Both steps can be difficult, but each one is equally necessary.

Surely by now we are all familiar with the trite little saying, "Pick your Battles," and have probably even repeated it a time or two to others when we see them having unnecessary battles with their own children, spouses, ex-spouses, or parents. A few years ago, there seemed to be a "pick your battles" movement winding its way throughout our Western society.

Even Dr. Phil, the renowned television psychologist, can frequently be heard repeating the phrase on his talk show, usually directing the simplistic wisdom toward families and parenting.

While it may be a true statement, it can become overwhelmingly mind-boggling to determine just which battles are worth picking and which battles are insignificant in the large scale of life and should be left alone. It's a no-brainer statement to spout off to friends and family, but it often becomes very difficult to execute in our own daily lives.

While one parent may think that a child's clothing must always be wrinkle-free, carefully matched (yes, that includes socks), and never worn more than one day in a row, another parent couldn't care less if their little darlings are running around wearing some horrendous outfit of black and orange looking like a gigantic

pumpkin (by the way moms, mismatched socks are now a hi popular fashion).

As moms, we usually want our kids to look clean and dressed, nicely groomed, and smelling fresh as a daisy. While seems like a relatively acceptable desire, have you ever a yourself why we want this? I have. The conclusion I have co is this. We want our children to look a certain way, act a ce way, and even smell a certain way, because we wrongly be that our darling children portray to the outside wo representation of ourselves.

Guess what? Our children do not represent us. They are own little individuals. They have their own minds, their ow and dislikes, and their own styles. The very best way for th discover who they are as individuals, separate from us, is them try out a few things (within reason, of course).

To my knowledge, it has never killed anyone to impers gigantic pumpkin for a day or two. While it certainly may our personal pride and cause us to whisper to the old snickering in the mall, "He dressed himself," it won't do an term, permanent damage to your children. This is certainl battle worth fighting.

If every single day throughout the entire summe eccentric young child wants to wear oversized rubber bo orange shorts and a green plaid button down shirt stuffe with an over filled pocket protector, that is okay. To you, h look like a crunchy little carrot, but to him he looks super is ready for whatever might come his way throughout th

By choosing this battle and forcing him to wear sand everyone else" or exchanging his orange shorts for c denim cut-offs "like his cousin Michael," you will ac stifling your child's sense of self and his creative abilitie not a battle worth fighting.

# BOUNDARIES & BATTLES

This chapter and the following one, "Consider Consistency," go hand in hand. Deciding which behaviours are worth battling for and which ones should be quietly overlooked is the initial step. The equally important secondary step is implementing your decisions with absolute consistency. Both steps can be difficult, but each one is equally necessary.

Surely by now we are all familiar with the trite little saying, "Pick your Battles," and have probably even repeated it a time or two to others when we see them having unnecessary battles with their own children, spouses, ex-spouses, or parents. A few years ago, there seemed to be a "pick your battles" movement winding its way throughout our Western society.

Even Dr. Phil, the renowned television psychologist, can frequently be heard repeating the phrase on his talk show, usually directing the simplistic wisdom toward families and parenting.

While it may be a true statement, it can become overwhelmingly mind-boggling to determine just which battles are worth picking and which battles are insignificant in the large scale of life and should be left alone. It's a no-brainer statement to spout off to friends and family, but it often becomes very difficult to execute in our own daily lives.

While one parent may think that a child's clothing must always be wrinkle-free, carefully matched (yes, that includes socks), and never worn more than one day in a row, another parent couldn't care less if their little darlings are running around wearing some horrendous outfit of black and orange looking like a gigantic

Life is hard. There is no end to the negative things we can choose to dwell on. Similarly, there is also no end to the positive things we can dwell on. The problem is that it is much easier to see the negative and to wallow in it. It is a pattern-a habit that we get into, whether it is learned behaviour that we are unaware of or we have just had a tough road and are in the habit of expecting bad things. The choice is yours—make it wisely. Remember, "*a wise woman builds her house.*"

There is good news, ladies—you can choose to step from the darkness of negativity into the light of positivity.

So it's simple. Choose to guard your thoughts carefully, because what you think on, you will speak on. We need to learn to control our minds, for it is there that the battles are won or lost. What comes out of our mouths is simply a by-product of what is living in our heads.

Words...

Choose them wisely. When there are no good, positive words to say, say nothing.

"*He who guards his lips guards his life, but he who speaks rashly will come to ruin.*" (Proverbs 13:3) pumpkin (by the way moms, mismatched socks are now a highly popular fashion).

As moms, we usually want our kids to look clean and well dressed, nicely groomed, and smelling fresh as a daisy. While this seems like a relatively acceptable desire, have you ever asked yourself why we want this? I have. The conclusion I have come to is this. We want our children to look a certain way, act a certain way, and even smell a certain way, because we wrongly believe that our darling children portray to the outside world a representation of ourselves.

Guess what? Our children do not represent us. They are their own little individuals. They have their own minds, their own likes and dislikes, and their own styles. The very best way for them to discover who they are as individuals, separate from us, is to let them try out a few things (within reason, of course).

To my knowledge, it has never killed anyone to impersonate a gigantic pumpkin for a day or two. While it certainly may wound our personal pride and cause us to whisper to the old ladies snickering in the mall, "He dressed himself," it won't do any long-term, permanent damage to your children. This is certainly not a battle worth fighting.

If every single day throughout the entire summer, your eccentric young child wants to wear oversized rubber boots with orange shorts and a green plaid button down shirt stuffed neatly with an over filled pocket protector, that is okay. To you, he might look like a crunchy little carrot, but to him he looks super cool and is ready for whatever might come his way throughout the day.

By choosing this battle and forcing him to wear sandals "like everyone else" or exchanging his orange shorts for cute little denim cut-offs "like his cousin Michael," you will actually be stifling your child's sense of self and his creative abilities. This is not a battle worth fighting.

Now, that is not to say that we never take an opportunity to teach. If it is becoming too much of a problem, then you certainly need to pick out three or four reasonable outfits and let him choose between them. By doing so, you are having some control while still allowing your child to have some choices. You both win a battle that was never fought.

Please don't misunderstand this and think that I am saying teenagers should be able to wear whatever they choose—they need serious boundaries in their older years. As our kids get older, us moms can encourage appropriate clothing styles—after all, it is us who slides that little piece of hard plastic through the machine and pray to God it doesn't ring a bell and scream "declined."

Let's be reasonable here. Our teenagers cannot wear what we won't buy them. We do get to have some say in such matters, but we must be absolutely sure that we are instilling appropriateness rather than our own personal styles. Teaching appropriateness and purity starts in the preschool years and must be introduced there. Once the teenage years are in full swing, we must reinforce what we have already taught them each and every time they attempt to push the limits or test the boundaries.

We cannot have our little girls wearing tiny little skirts with their bottoms hanging out and then expect that when they are thirteen and fourteen they will suddenly have an inner knowledge of appropriateness. Furthermore, we absolutely must teach by example. We cannot expect our daughters to wear tops that cover their chests if we are walking around with cleavage to our belly buttons (quite honestly, after we've had a few children, everything eventually ends up around our belly button). It is up to us moms to model modesty and appropriateness in clothing. These are the things that we must be ready to battle if the time presents itself. Modesty and appropriateness is a battle worth fighting for.

Similarly, later on in our children's lives, this personal creativity may turn into undesirable piercings or gothic attire, and you certainly must have the final say in such matters. This is definitely a battle worth fighting. When my own son came to me at sixteen and asked if he could get his lip pierced, my answer was yes. However, that answer came with some restrictions and numerous conditions. I chose not to have a battle, but rather strategically lay out enough guidelines to make the choice very difficult for any young man—and my son, in particular.

My son was very responsible, working a part-time job while pulling in straight A's in high school. He had already purchased a car and was fully responsible for his own gas money, registration, and all the costs that come with owning a vehicle.

Because he had proven to be responsible, and had a long history of making good decisions, and because I had known so many kids who did not bother asking but rather went out and got something pierced only to have the fight later with their mother or father, I had to give my son the respect he had earned.

My answer went something like this, "You may get your lip pierced, but you must pay for it yourself, and if it gets infected you must remove it." Furthermore, if people stared or made rude comments, my son was not allowed to be angry or annoyed because, after all, if you make a decision that is going to cause people to stare or make rude comments, you certainly cannot be upset when those things happen. Finally, if this new facial decoration caused any issues for his teeth whatsoever, it must come out.

He did eventually decide to get the hole punched into his lip, but quickly admitted it was not worth the money he had to pay for it. It didn't last very long and he took it out, saying it was "kinda dumb."

If I would have turned it into a major battle and forbid him to get it done, adding all kinds of ridiculous threats and comments, he might not have gotten a hole punched into his lip at that time, but neither would he have had the opportunity to learn any of life's valuable lessons. He realized it was "kinda dumb" all on his own, without mom having to tell him. While I did have the final say, rather than just say no, I chose to instill some boundaries that we both could live with.

He learned some responsibility, realized he had wasted his hard-earned cash, and understood that his mom trusted him enough to make a choice. He learned that he could calmly come to his mom and expect to have a rational conversation—not a battle. Next time he needs advice or an opinion, chances are he will again come to me because he knows that I will listen and not turn his questions into a battle that I must win.

It is believed that when our children are very young, it's a bit easier to decide which battles to walk into and which ones to avoid. I believe differently. If we pick our battles very carefully when our children are younger, taking every possible teaching opportunity and continue to be consistent in all things, when our pudgy-cheeked little darlings evolve into these strange beings whom we fear and call teenagers, we will have already instilled good and proper values into them and the battles will not be often, or difficult.

Think about this—do you really want your child to grow up to be "just like everyone else?" Wouldn't you prefer your children to emerge into adulthood with their own minds and thoughts and creativity and individuality? So often when they are young, we try to conform them to be "like everyone else." When they get older and want to do things that everyone else is doing, we say, "Why don't you just be yourself?" The sad truth is that very often, we have not allowed them to discover who they are, so we cannot expect them to know who they are.

## Age Appropriate Battles

Children need age-appropriate boundaries and freedoms. It is very dangerous to expect things from our kids which they are unable to follow through on. We as moms must take a deep breath and sometimes a hard look into our own hearts to determine why we desire particular actions from our children. We all desire for our children to behave and act appropriately in every situation, and while that is unrealistic, we must ask ourselves why we desire this in the first place. Is it for the benefit of our children or for the benefit of us moms?

Especially as single moms, we want the world to see us as super parents. We don't want to fit into that "typical single mom" statistic where the kids are out of control. I fell into the trap and I bet you did too—at least for a little while. "My kids are going to behave just so the rest of the world knows that kids can be raised without a dad and still turn out wonderfully." While this is a true statement, we take it too personally and unfairly pass unrealistic expectations on to our children. Often, we single moms become too hard on our children because we want to prove to ourselves, our families, and society that we can do it on our own. We want to prove them all wrong!

What are age appropriate boundaries? Let's start with the chubby cheeks and snotty noses of preschool.

## Preschool

There are not many boundaries at this young age, but the ones we do choose to focus on must be done with absolute consistency in order to firmly establish a trust factor for the rest of your parenting career. At this innocent young age, we must equip our children with what is needed for when that day comes they move from pre-schooler to the "big girl who's in grade one." It is in these preschool years where we have the ability to empower our little ones to be able to function in the outside world, out from under the ever watchful eyes and protection of mommy. Boundaries here include truth telling, obedience to those in authority (mommy), and absolute trust. When mommy says no, it means no. This must be an irrevocable boundary at the preschool age, because this is the age where children will dangerously run into the street to retrieve their favourite ball or sneak away from mom in the grocery store in search of the candy aisle. The consequences need not be harsh, however they must be consistently carried out. It only takes once for a child to not listen to mommy's "no" and run into the street in front of a car. Instilling a healthy fear into children at this age is necessary because kids are not born with fears. Now, I can hear you saying, "I don't want my child to learn fear," but the Bible indicates that there is a healthy fear. Fear of the Lord, for example. It is necessary to teach healthy fears of moving cars or strangers. This is the age when we can introduce them to healthy fear so that when they are older we can tell them to do or not do something and they will listen to us because we have taught them to trust us. These are the battles worth fighting. Bedtime is also a battle worth fighting at this young age since it often tends to be problematic, especially for preschoolers of single moms. This is because we as moms are tired by 8:00 pm and just want to relax. While it is so easy to just let our little angels fall asleep on our laps as we flick through the meaningless television stations, in the long run it is not a good area to loosen up our boundaries. If we choose to let our weariness get the best of us right now, we will quickly have a school-aged child who refuses to go to bed and will have unwittingly created a very big battle. It will be an every night of the week fight, which we will most often lose because we are too tired. What was easy at four years old is no longer easy at eight. Carrying a thirty pound sleeping beauty down the hall to her bed is exponentially easier than carrying an eighty pound deadweight fourth grader down that same hall. Simply get a routine for your child and habitually go through that routine every single night. Before long, your sweet preschooler will learn the habit of bedtime and you will have just saved yourself, and your child, years of frustrating bedtime battles.

It does not necessarily matter what your bedtime routine is with your preschooler; just get one and stick to it. For my own sons, it went something like this...

• Have a nice warm bath and play for a little while in the bubbles.

• Get out, dry off, attempt to slick the little wisps of hair down and put on pajamas.

• Enjoy a snack and a chat with mom about whatever happy things went on that day.

• Stop at the toilet on the way to their bedroom to do "bathroom stuff."

• Fill the water bottle with fresh cool water—just enough for a few sips lest they have to sneak to the toilet a hundred times.

• Move the Kleenex box from the dresser to the night table.

• Move the garbage can from across the room to beside the bed, because at bedtime children decide to actually use the wastebasket for their five barely used Kleenexes.

• Pull back the covers and help the boys crawl into their beds.

• Tuck their blankets around them.

• Read them a favourite story.

• Say a prayer.

• Kiss them.

• Tell them I love them and enjoyed them very much that day.

• Say good night.

With that, I would exit the room, leaving the door open just a crack and whisper back, "I'll see you in the morning." Now, this little routine did not guarantee that one of the boys would not attempt to sneak out within minutes of my sitting down in my favourite overstuffed rocker and settling in to watch an hour or so of meaningless television. At first, this happened frequently and they would have all kinds of things they "needed to tell me." Each time, without fail, I would quietly take their little hand and assure them they could tell me their emergency in the morning. After that, we would walk silently down the hall back to their room. I would pull the blankets back, have them crawl in, and say good night. Nothing more, nothing less. We cannot engage them in conversation at this point or we have just lost the battle. Sometimes I would have to walk them back to their rooms five or six times in an evening, but they quickly learned that they were not winning. They were also not making mommy angry or getting her attention or getting her to talk to them...so eventually they just gave up.

After a few weeks of this scene, the sneaking out of their beds quickly declined and they learned nothing was going to change. Like magic, the bedtime was established. By the time they were old enough to go to school, bathe and dress themselves, my part in their bedtime routine was all of ten minutes. I could relax in the evening knowing they were not going to be wandering in and out of the living room and were getting a good night's sleep, getting up in the morning refreshed and ready for a great day. This is a battle well worth investing time in during the preschool years so you don't have to fight the battle in their later years. Believe me, a bedtime battle with an eleven or twelve-year-old is much more difficult, time-consuming, and frustrating than a little battle with a four-year-old. Establish these little things now so they don't become big things later and turn into endless battles.

## Elementary School

If we have already instilled honesty, obedience, and trust into our children during their preschool years, we are way ahead of most families. Now that our children are heading to school, we can add some new age appropriate boundaries while continuing to be consistent with the ones already established. Don't be fooled—every now and then our kids will attempt to push those boundaries and test us. Be very careful to reaffirm that those boundaries still apply. Remember, when choosing which boundaries to implement into our home, that they are not there so that we can be controlling or have "the last say," or so we can look like super mom to the rest of the block. Boundaries are never for us—they are always for teaching our children to become responsible adults who much too quickly become an active part of society outside the safety net of our homes. It is within those safe secure walls of our home where our children are going to learn life's valuable tools. It is our job to train our children for life.

Some boundaries you may want to consider putting in place during these elementary school years are:

• Homework comes before playing.

• Always do your best. If you have done your best work, it does not matter what the letter on your report card says. C's are acceptable if it's to the best of your ability. If you can't get your blankets to be just right on your bed, a few wrinkles is just fine if you tried your best.

• No bullying anybody, ever—not the kids at school, brothers, neighbours, or that annoying brat down the street. This includes bullying of every kind—name calling, cyber bullying, physical bullying, and anything else that falls under the word. I am sure that you will think of other boundaries that will be necessary for your children, but these three in particular teach personal responsibility, respect for others and respect for self—the most crucial life lessons for our children. If we can instill these values into our children, our battles will be few and far between. When there is need for a battle to be fought, it will be short-lived, because you have already instilled the most crucial values to your children. If you can implement these few boundaries into your elementary grade children, you are absolutely on the right track towards raising respectful, wonderful children. When you are setting such boundaries, ensure that you communicate these in an age appropriate manner to your children, as well as the consequences if they choose to move outside one of the boundaries.

As your children get older, the boundaries that you set must be clear. They must be age appropriate and be communicated to your children in a manner which they absolutely understand. When you are talking to them, ensure they are listening by having them repeat back what you've said. By making eye contact and having them repeat it back to you, you avoid the far too common "But I didn't hear you" battle. Above all, when your children choose to step out of the boundaries you have set for them, follow through with the consequences.

There are likely hundreds of things that you could come up with to create battles over, but often these are nothing more than personal preferences; leave these things alone. Your children are not you.

They may look like you and sound like you and walk like you but they are not you. They have their own preferences and their own minds, so if they forget to put their glass in the dishwasher once in a while or doodle on their school binders, don't sweat it. If they are forgetful or a bit absentminded once in a while, don't sweat it. If they leave their bed unmade or are a bit late getting to bed once in a while, don't sweat it. We've all heard the saying, "Don't sweat the small stuff," and it's so true—especially with kids. Sweating isn't all that attractive anyway.

Look instead for teaching opportunities. When you ask sweet little fourteen-year-old Madeline to clean her room and she miraculously goes to her room and shuts the door, assume she's cleaning her room. When she retreats from that same room only moments later, don't be surprised that every single thing that was previously on the floor, dresser or bed is now suspiciously out of sight. The now-made bed will probably be an inch or two higher than it was yesterday and with a quick glance you will likely see the items from the floor shoved safely under the bed. Not a battle to pick, but an amazing opportunity to teach.

It won't be long before sweet Madeline wants her clothes ironed or washed because everything she owns is shoved under the bed—not great for wrinkles or smell. This is a perfect opportunity to say no. Believe it or not, saying no is healthy for children and teenagers and we do *not* need to feel guilty for that wonderful little two-letter word. We need to practice it and learn to be very comfortable saying it.

Now, none of us wants our beautiful young ladies to go to school smelling badly or looking as though they have worn their clothes to bed because it might make us look bad as moms. However, if you say no to her request to wash all her clothes or try to get the peanut butter out of her favourite jeans (coincidentally, one should never shove a half-eaten peanut butter sandwich and clothes under the same bed), she will most likely be angry with you. She might even tell you that you are a terrible mother or maybe even the worst mother on the entire planet—and that's okay. This is not a battle worth fighting. Simply, and in a very calm tone, remind her that it is not you who's wearing peanut butter to work, because you took a few moments to throw your sandwich in the trash, and you took another few moments to put your clothes away. Unfortunately, Madeline chose another option—shoving everything under the bed—and that option has some rather unfortunate outcomes.

Saying yes in such situations would be over parenting and when we over parent, we actually disable the natural consequences that are so important for our children to learn. Repeat after me: "I am not my child's property to be demanded about. I do not have a string attached to me, so I must stop letting my child pull me around."

When our darlings make silly choices, they need to feel the repercussions of those choices. But remind them that the consequences are natural ones which they brought on themselves. You have nothing to do with it. Remember, all children must learn that there are natural consequences for choices and that they are responsible for them, not you. It is not your responsibility to dig them out of every hole they ever get into or every situation they don't like. These are not your battles to fight.

A great opportunity has created itself to teach Madeline the importance of taking care of her things. It makes no difference to you if she shoves everything under her bed because you don't have to wear wrinkled tops or peanut buttered jeans. Things like this may seem cruel, but moms, face it: if we hop to the beat of our children's drums, we'll get very dizzy and end up falling down. On the other hand, if we back off and let them fall down once in a while, they will quickly learn to make better choices, become personally responsible, and grow into the wonderful self-controlled adults we so desire them to be.

While we don't need to make everything a battle, we do need to allow them to feel the natural consequences of their own silly actions and poor choices. If we don't allow this now, when they are older they will not have learned to take responsibility for their own actions and choices; every problem for the rest of their lives will be somebody else's fault. Remember, mom, it is not our job to be our children's friends. They already have friends, and likely so do you. What they need is a mother who will be strong enough to say no when it is in their best interest, even if that means your sweet darling child will not like you for it. Ephesians 6:4 warns against parents exasperating their children and instructs us instead to "bring them up in the training and admonition of the Lord" (NKJV). I often wonder if this 'exasperation' refers to picking up battles that should be left alone.

# CONSIDER CONSISTENCY

All good parenting books have one common thread woven meticulously throughout their pages. That priceless thread is called consistency! It was the key to excellent parenting when we were kids, and it's still the key to quality parenting and well-developed, well-balanced kids today.

"Consistent to what?" you might say. "Consistent in everything." is my response. Often, we single moms want to let our kids get away with just a little because of our own self-inflicted guilt. We feel bad because they are coping without a father or they've just gotten back from dad's house and are a bit moody now. We tend to give our children excuses to behave badly and by doing so we are certainly not doing them any favours. In fact, by giving them excuses to behave badly we are reinforcing the bad behaviour and we can expect it to continue.

The truth is that before we can implement consistency, we must first seriously contemplate our own personal beliefs and decide what it is that we want to instil into our children. What is it that we believe so much that we need our children to carry it into adulthood? What is it that we want our children to know and learn and instil into their own lives? What areas do we nag in today so that eventually, when we are no longer there to nag them, our dear children will do on their own, without even thinking about it?

I believe these areas are basically the same for every parent and include things such as respecting themselves and respecting others. Within the boundaries of those two basic desires come more concrete issues such as lying, disobeying those in authority, and stealing.

There are basic life principles that we need to instil into our children. The most valuable of those principles is that all choices have consequences; good choices produce good consequences and wrong choices produce painful and undesired consequences.

This is not something some grouchy demanding mean mother made up: it is a life principle—like gravity. It is that way just because it is an unchangeable principle. All other areas fall within the parameters of this one cosmic truth of "choices and consequences." This is even a Biblical principle, as we can see throughout scripture. Specifically and very simply put, *"Do not be deceived: God cannot be mocked. A man reaps what he sows"* (Galatians 6:7).

There are three basic keys to consistency. If we will spend the time considering and implementing consistency into our homes, lives, and children's lives, we will guarantee that life in general is just that much simpler and safer.

Key #1—Decide which negative behaviours are absolutely unacceptable and which positive behaviours we are responsible for instilling into our little darlings.

An excellent place to look for positive personal attributes is the Word of God. His Word lists things like honesty and obedience, compassion and sexual morality, kindness and trustworthiness. It is when we dig into His word that we can determine what things we need, as a parent, to teach our children. In the big picture, we are giving our children priceless, non-returnable gifts that will bless them and enable them to live adult lives that are both positive and beneficial.

It is in God's Word where we can get a picture of what it is God expects from His children. Philippians 4:8, for example, tells us to dwell on things that are *true, noble, right, lovely, admirable, excellent, and praiseworthy*. Obviously, being dishonest, stealing, and bullying are not going to fit anywhere into this list.

73

Galatians 5:22 lists the fruits of the Spirit which, if we are living according to the will and plan of God, we will possess and want our children to possess as well. This list includes *love, joy, peace, patience, kindness, goodness, and self-control.* When we are meditating on what we value and want to instil into our children, we must carefully meditate on this list and see how our desires for our children fit into these desires of God.

Remember, while there are plenty of negative, harmful behaviours we want to keep our children from, there are also plenty of positive behaviours that we want them to internalize for their future happiness and fulfillment. These two lists from Scripture very simply lay out what those positive things need to be.

Let's look at a few practical examples of how to be consistent when our children choose to step out of the boundaries we have lovingly set for them.

It's a great principle to teach our children obedience. When they are tiny adorable little creatures with pinchable cheeks and runny noses, it's tough to discipline for small acts of disobedience. We ask little Johnny not to eat the cookies right before supper because they are for dessert and of course, as all good moms know, if little Johnny eats cookies right before supper it will ruin his little appetite. Seems reasonable, right?

Inevitably the phone rings, and in that millisecond that mom turns her back to run to the phone, a cookie disappears and, coincidentally, so does little Johnny. You giggle, hang up the phone and call for everyone to gather round the table for supper. Sure enough, here comes little Johnny with a mouth overflowing with chocolate drool and brown sweetness smeared across his pudgy little face.

While swallowing an outburst of laughter, it is painfully apparent to us that sweet little Johnny has chosen to disobey. This seems like such a minor issue and, after all, he is as cute as can be with his sheepish chocolaty grin stretching from ear to ear. You really should be running for your camera, but you must focus on the act of disobedience and not the toothless grin staring up at you.

The Lord firmly tells us parents that *"He who spares the rod hates his son, but he who loves him is careful to discipline him"* (Proverbs 13:24). While there have been theologians, psychologists and parents arguing over this "rod" for hundreds of years, I believe that we can insert the word "discipline" for that little word, "rod."

The point is not whether it is a literal rod or whether it is referring to corporal punishment. The point is that we cannot spare our children discipline. If we love our children, we must be very careful to be consistent in our discipline.

Disobedience is disobedience. There's no way around it. If the instruction was clear and the child understood what you were saying, then any act of disobedience requires consistent discipline. Whether we are a believer in spankings or time outs or taking away privileges, I'll guarantee you one thing: if we are consistent in the discipline of our children, they will quickly learn to weigh the expected consequence with the considered action.

They may still choose to disobey once in a while, but with absolute consistency, we will see a quick decline in the undesirable action. Discipline may not be harsh for such an action as poor little Johnny's disobedience, but believe me, children learn things whether we teach them or not.

Lack of concrete, age appropriate discipline for this act of disobedience will most definitely teach Johnny something we do not want him to learn. With inconsistent discipline, Johnny will learn that he can get away with disobeying mommy if he's cute enough. This sets him up for big problems later in his life. He will see the act of obeying as his choice rather than an expectation. He will also wonder why, when his disobedience does get him into trouble, he is not cute enough to get out of it this time.

Key #2—Decide which consequences fit which behaviours, both positive and negative.

Once you decide what is intolerable behaviour for you child, such as disobedience, lying, aggression, cursing, or stealing, you can move toward this second key and begin to construct your own process of consequences. Just as children of all ages need very specific boundaries, they also need very specific responses to the breaking of those boundaries.

Key #2 requires us to spend some time thinking and praying about the consequences for the undesired actions. Consequences do not need to be the same for every wrong action, but they do need to remain the same within their action (as long as they are age appropriate). Let me explain. When my children chose to tell me a lie, we would sit down and briefly discuss it.

After we agreed that they had lied and determined their reason for doing so, we would take a short walk to the bathroom where I had a not-so-pleasant bar of soap. Surprisingly, they would willingly stick their little tongues out and allow me to rub the tiniest bit of the bar onto it. Not enough to hurt them, but enough to help them realize that their lie certainly did not make the consequence worthwhile.

They would continue, every now and then, to try and sneak a little lie past old mom, and each time they met the same consequence. If I had let my soft heart deter me from using that bar of soap for even one lie, I would have taught them that sometimes their lies have consequences and sometimes they don't. So all I'd really be teaching them is confusion and uncertainty. Now that they are older, I can say with certainty that they are truth tellers and they find value in truth from others as well.

While soap on the tongue was the expected consequence for telling a lie, it was not the expected consequence for coming home late, because quite frankly that would be silly and make no sense. We must ensure that the consequence fits the action.

When my sons got older and responsible enough to venture out on their own or with friends, they were always given a specific time to be home. They understood that it was in their best interest to be on time; so much so that most often they arrived home early just to be sure they were within the boundaries I had laid out. They knew beyond a shadow of a doubt that if they arrived home late, they certainly would not be going out with friends or for any other reason for the rest of the week.

It did not make any difference what was happening that they were going to have to miss. Whether a hockey game or a friend's pool party, if they were late on Thursday, they would not be going to either the game or the party on Friday or Saturday. They knew that because of consistency. If mom said it, that's how it was going to be!

Now, we cannot be so rigid that there is never room for understanding. Because, time is a thing that is concrete, and our clocks may all be a bit off. Giving a five-minute grace period is a good idea, simply because the clock on your living room wall may be a few minutes different from the clock on your child's wrist—or cell phone. Giving that few minute leeway says that while you are helping your child stay within the boundaries set out, you are also willing to give a little because of circumstances (such as different clocks reading different times).

Here is a warning—do not let your darling child talk you into a ten-minute grace period (if your clocks are that much off, you should get a new clock) because if you do, before long it will be fifteen minutes, then twenty minutes, and on and on. Remember, you get to set the boundaries. Your child gets to decide whether or not to live within those boundaries, knowing that if he chooses to step outside of them, there will be a cost.

Key #3—the follow through.

There is good news to this consequence thing. Along with consistency in discipline and consequences comes consistency in good and positive things. We often make promises to our children, usually so we can bribe them into behaving and allowing us some peace and quiet. These promises need to be followed through on—always. Short of an absolute disaster, we must concretely follow through on positive consequences. This is how children learn to trust us, and ultimately trust God.

If we want our children to believe us when we lay down consequences for wrong behaviour we must prove to them that we are trustworthy and will follow through. A person cannot be trustworthy only sometimes, because by default that makes them untrustworthy. If we want our children to trust us, we must show them that we can be trusted. If we promised them a birthday party then without doubt we throw them a birthday party. Never promise something that is out of your control to deliver upon.

When the children are young, we go to the store for a "quick stop." We say to little Suzie, "Now Suzie, when mommy is all done, I will get you a treat at the counter." Now that you've said it, you must do it. Whether little Suzie screams like a crazy person or throws a tantrum or is the most delightful little person in the store, you absolutely must get her a treat at the counter. You said you would.

Of course, we do not need to give the treat to Suzie at that very moment. You might let her pick out a treat and watch you purchase it before calmly sticking it into your bag, saying, "Suzie, mommy bought you that treat because I said I would, and when you decide to stop yelling and act like my sweet little Suzie again, I will certainly love to give the treat to you. Until you decide to do that, mommy will be happy to hold onto the treat for you."

Oh, the screaming may get louder, but you stuck to your word. You were consistent and Suzie will know that. She will also know that she cannot act poorly without it costing her something.

Of course, most of us frazzled moms tend to say instead, "Suzie, if you behave and are a good little girl, mommy will give you a treat at the counter." Never bribe a child to behave in such a way that should be expected behaviour. I am going to suggest we save this little nugget of value called "the bribe" for situations much more demanding, which we will discuss in a few moments.

If Suzie was throwing a tantrum at the store and you indicated to her that when you got home, Suzie was going to have to spend fifteen minutes in her bedroom and go without the anticipated dessert of scrumptious smelling warm chocolate cake you had just put into your cart, then when you get home, ensure that those things happen.

If little Suzie knows from experience that she can misbehave in the store and you will forget about it or be too tired to carry out the threatened action once home, you can be guaranteed that Suzie will act out in public more often than she will behave in public—just because she can.

If, on the other hand, Suzie learns that when she acts out in public, mom will leave her cart and take Suzie home to bed with no snack, mom will soon be able to have confidence that she can take Suzie to the store and expect her to behave just like a little angel because Suzie knows she must.

Mom is in control of the boundaries at all times. Just as soon as little Suzie learns this truth, both Suzie and mom will have a better relationship because each knows the boundaries and the absolute consequences of stepping outside those boundaries. Trust has been formed and there is always a security within the walls of that trust.

I recall one such shopping trip with one of my sons. He did not want to be in the particular store and insisted on throwing his bag of animal cookies onto the floor. After the second time of me scooping up the bag and returning it to him, I looked him right in his big blue eyes and said, "If you choose to throw the cookies on the floor again, they are going to go into the garbage."

Of course he decided to test the limits I had just set out before him, and with one final toss, the cookies landed right at my feet. Like a good mommy, I picked up the crackers and calmly asked the cashier to throw the candy into the trash basket.

As my son watched his bag of cookies disappear, his eyes grew big and spat at me (oh yes, he did). Without hesitation, I flicked his cute little lips and he began to cry. He was not hurt, nor was he shocked, because he knew that if he decided to spit at me, his lip would feel a quick little stinging flick.

At that instant in my peripheral vision, I spotted two ladies walking towards me. The first told me angrily that I was a horrible mother if I thought it was okay to flick my child's lips. My response to her was "Would you like him to spit at you?" She promptly ejected a sharp-tongued "Well of course not" from her own pursed lips. I sweetly replied, "And he won't—because he now knows that spitting at people causes his lips to sting."

She walked away speechless and somewhat horrified. The other lady came to me, patted me on the arm and said, "Way to go. It's too bad more parents won't discipline their children. It's a lack of what you just did that is making this world such a disrespectful place to live." Now, there were two ladies with very different responses to me. I can guess with almost certainty which one of those older ladies has well-mannered respectful children and which has children that none of us would want to be around.

We cannot be afraid to discipline our children. It is not to save our pride or for our own benefit, but for the long-term benefit of our precious children. If we let fear of what other people might think cause us to back off and be inconsistent with our children, we will be causing damage to them.

Again, children learn something from every situation. They are so smart. Our kids will immediately learn that mommy is too afraid to discipline them in public, so guess where our precious little darlings will act up? You got it—in public.

I hope you are now seeing how consistency is a wide blanket which covers all areas of parenting. Consistency means "unchanging." It means that once we have said something, whatever that something is, we must follow through.

Because we are imperfect creatures, we will make mistakes. We become frustrated and spew out ridiculous threats when our child is acting out, threats which both we and our kids know we will never carry out. We must then take that threat back and apologize for our outburst. It is not in making the mistakes where we fail, but in our unwillingness to acknowledge and take responsibility for those mistakes.

## The Bribe

The bribe is a unique and universal tool that should be kept under lock and key in a very sacred place, taken out only for those special occasions when we believe that we absolutely *must* have our child's cooperation for their best interest.

Us moms often find it very easy to bribe our kids for the most minute things. "If you go to bed like a good little girl tonight, mommy will let you have fruit loops for breakfast." Or how about, "If you will be good in the store while mommy's shopping, I will buy you a milkshake when we are done."

Don't get me wrong, it's not the worst parenting error in the world (and every parent on the planet is guilty of it), however the bribe should be used very sparingly. If we overuse the bribe, we are teaching our kids to do things or act a certain way in order to gain something. While this certainly might work to gain the desired behaviour, if it is overused we create little monsters.

Our children will begin to do things such as simply behaving only to "gain something." There are certain behaviours that are just expected. Going to bed on time and without coming to the kitchen for seventeen sips of water, for example, should be expected and not subject to rewards.

We should never bribe our children to perform expected behaviours such as going to bed. If you ask your ten-year-old child to do a simple task, such as pick up his toys or make his bed, and his response is, "What are you going to give me if I do?" you have definitely overused the bribe and have given your sweet child the power. No, the bribe should definitely not be a regular occurrence.

My oldest son Riley is a remarkably talented musician. He took piano lessons for a number of years, and when he was nine years old he won a national song writing competition. Regardless of how talented he is, he absolutely refused to play in public—even at the spring recital which he'd worked hard all year to prepare for.

For his first spring recital, this talented little boy had his piece memorized perfectly, adding his little fortes and fortissimos. He was dressed over the top and had his hair slicked back just right. Even so, when his name was called to perform his piece, he absolutely refused to go to the piano. Horrified, I realized that all eyes had turned towards a panicked mother (me) and this cute little boy who was loudly screaming, "I'm not going."

I recognized this as a losing battle and certainly not one I was willing to play out in front of a hundred staring eyes. The gracious and slightly embarrassed piano teacher, Mrs. Hagan, smiled nervously and said, "Well, perhaps at the end of the recital we can hear Riley's piece."

"Fat Chance!" I mumbled loud enough to spark some giggles from the parents around me. Well, my son did not play his piece that day. Turns out, even though he was talented and prepared, he was absolutely terrified of an audience. There was nothing I could have done that day to make him change his mind.

The next year, however, turned out quite differently. As Spring Recital was quickly approaching and my little Riley was practicing his heart out mastering every note, rest, and repeat sign,

I asked him if he thought he would be able to overcome his fear this year and play his piece. He immediately responded with, "I am not going to play it."

After a hefty sigh, I got some professional advice. Yes, I called my own mother, who happens to be a piano teacher. She had experienced a similar problem with some of her own students and gave me a suggestion I found odd, but certainly worth a try. My brilliant mother suggested I tape a $20 bill to the refrigerator door and tell my son that if he played at the recital, the money would be his. But if he chose not to play at the recital, the money would just stay stuck to the refrigerator door. The choice was completely his.

It was just that simple. I did not have to beg, plead, demand, reprimand, and my relationship with my son continued to be excellent because I quit nagging him. The $20 was certainly a bribe. I gave him nearly a month to stare at that money pinned to the fridge and contemplate what it was going to cost him to earn it.

He had time to think about it, ponder it, and when his name was called that spring recital afternoon, he chose to overcome his fear of an audience in order to earn that money. He made a mess of the piece, because he was so nervous his little fingers wouldn't stay on the keys, but he did it. That was his first step in overcoming his fears.

We went home and he proudly walked over to the refrigerator and took down the $20 that he had earned. He did not get money for playing in a recital ever again, because he had learned to overcome his fear. (That alone was worth the $20).

The following year, and every year since, he has walked calmly to the piano and played his pieces with pride and excellence, knowing there was nothing on the fridge for him. He had earned much more than $20 that day, he had earned self confidence, pride, and peace. Now that was a good bribe.

You see, ladies, the bribe has a special place. It is not to gain proper behaviour because proper behaviour should be consistently expected. The bribe is not to allow mommy a few moments of sanity, which is just an unrealistic dream. Rather, the bribe is used to teach our child a life skill or lesson. In my son's case, it was to overcome fear.

If he had not chosen to play his piece that day, the $20 would have remained taped to the refrigerator for the entire year until the next spring recital. The bribe was not to get Riley to play a piano piece: he and I both knew he could do that beautifully.

The bribe was to get him to choose to overcome his fear because that was something he didn't think he could do. He proved to himself that he could and now he does many things he likely would never have done if he had continued to live in fear of what people thought.

*"Let us not become weary in doing good, for at the proper time we will reap a harvest if we do not give up"* (Galatians 6:9). This means consistency, moms. Let's not grow weary in being consistent with our children, because in due season we will all reap a great harvest.

Parenting is a difficult task for a family who has a mother and a father, but doing it alone raises the bar exponentially. When we have to be both the mom and the dad, the good cop and the bad cop, the nice parent and the evil parent, it seems hopeless. None of us enjoy disciplining our children. I remember my father saying to me, "This is going to hurt me more than it's going to hurt you," and I remember thinking, "I doubt that very much."

It didn't take me long as a parent of my own precious children to realize that my father's words were exactly true. It does hurt a parent to discipline their children. It upsets us moms when we have to see our kids angry at us because they are grounded from their best friend's birthday party.

Us moms don't like being the "bad guy," but as a single mom, we are often the only "guy" around. We must effectively play both the good guy and the bad guy—often simultaneously. There was not one time that I got any pleasure or satisfaction whatsoever from rubbing a bar of soap on my sons' tongues. Most often I'd leave them leaning over the sink spitting bubbles and running cold water over their sour tongues, and go to my own bedroom and have a little cry.

We know it is in their best interests. Someone just yesterday asked me what I would do today if my sons (now nearly grown) lied to me, and without even having to think about it, I quickly responded, "They don't lie." I am so proud of them today for being honest, upstanding young men, and I know that if I had not been consistent in showing them that lying was never acceptable, I would not have such an assurance today that they are truth tellers.

I have recently spent some time with my oldest son, now nineteen years of age, when we were able to sit down and have an honest heart-to-heart dialogue. The topic was parenting. I sincerely asked him where I had messed up and where I did okay. He brilliantly told me that nobody likes discipline—especially kids. However, he knew that I was "being a mom" and that he had turned out pretty good because I had done my mom job well.

Buck up, moms…discipline hurts, but only for a short time. Do not give up, no matter how difficult it becomes, because the Lord promises us that we (and our children) will reap a harvest in due time. I believe that I am now reaping some of that harvest when I watch my sons consistently make excellent choices, even when their friends aren't. That harvest is bringing me pleasure when I see my sons acting with integrity and honesty, when they see someone less fortunate than them and they reach out a helping hand. Believe me when I say, the reward of the harvest is well worth the sacrifices.

Hebrews 12:11 assures as that "*no discipline seems pleasant at the time, but painful. Later on, however, it produces a harvest of righteousness and peace for those who have been trained by it.*" We are doing our children a lifelong favour by planting the seeds of consistent discipline into their lives so that later on, they too will reap a harvest.

# Section Three—Family Matters

Proverbs 14:1—The wise woman builds her house, but with her own hands the foolish one tears hers down.

Family is precious. We spend so much of our time trying to be all things to all people, but it's time for us to slow down and enjoy what matters most—our family. You will get out exactly what you put in. Build your house, mom, not with material possessions and beautiful things, but with joy, laughter, intimacy, and respect. You will reap exactly what you sow-therefore sow thoughtfully with joy.

# FAMILY TIME

Why is it that when Parker Brothers or Hasbro comes out with a brand new board game, the commercials to advertise their new product are always set in the early 80s? You know what I'm talking about. The boys with their Brill cream and pocket protectors and moms with their aprons and beehive up-dos? The nerdy little kids have plastic smiles glued to their faces while swooning, "Oh Johnny, that was a really great turn."

I watch these commercials and giggle, but wonder why they make them that way. I pondered this question for quite some time before coming up with an answer. With the increase of technology, the breakdown of family, and everyone's time being silently stolen, these scenes from television commercials are but a distant memory.

Parker Brothers and Hasbro are brilliant, really, stirring up such fond memories in hopes of lighting a spark within the hearts of nostalgic mothers. Those are the ones who go out and buy their games, take them home full of excitement hoping to relive some of their own childhood through such games, and then set them on the shelf to collect dust.

The bottom line is that these scenes just don't happen in today's homes anymore. Twenty years ago, perhaps we could peak through any living room window on a Friday evening and see the family gathered around the coffee table rolling dice and squealing in delight. Today, however, this is not a scene that can be easily found. It's up to you and I to change the scenery and make it one that plays out in our own living rooms regularly. It's called family time.

Making such a suggestion often induces sheer terror and the gnashing of teeth—especially for single parents. If you have not experienced positive family times, you may be thinking, "Family time? With *my* family? Absolutely not." However, family time can be very fun and is a key to creating well-adjusted and close relationships between not only you and your children but also between one child and another.

Family time is *not* when two or three of you are sitting in the same room with one watching television, one texting, and still another reading a book. That is simply a few people sitting in the same room sharing air.

I recall being newly married and whining (yes, I was a whiner) to my husband on a regular basis, "I want you to spend time with me—you are never around." He would quickly reply with, "What do you mean I'm never around? I have been in the garage all day long!" I, of course, being the sweet, quiet, well-mannered little wife that I was way back then, would storm away yelling, "Just because you're on the property does *not* mean you're spending time with me."

I always lost that argument, but the truth remains. Just because you are in the same house does not mean you are spending time together. People can be in the same room and not spend time together. Family time must be intentional or it will not work.

Creating positive family time can be tricky, especially if there is a large age gap between your children or if your kids have varied interests, but it is not impossible. It can be a time of learning and sharing and of giving in and not always having things done one person's way. Planting seeds of quality family time will produce a harvest for years—and generations—to come.

There are numerous ways to incorporate family time and you will likely come up with some that are not mentioned here. There is no one particular "method" that works better than another. However, there are a few guidelines which need to be understood by everyone—especially you.

When your family is having some together time that is allotted just for that, all cell phones, laptops, and iPods (and whatever other neat little time-consuming gadgets have been invented by the time you read this book) must be shut off. Not on vibrate, or mute, or set over on the counter, but off.

Contrary to popular knowledge, absolutely every single one of these gadgets has an off button. It might be tough to locate it at first, or figure out just which way to switch the tiny little button, but believe me, there is an off button—find it, have your kids find it, and then use it. This means you too, mom. You cannot expect your kids to do something that you yourself are not willing to do. Kids learn by our example, so model good skills and turn your gadgets off.

It will be rough at first and the kids will likely be angry. You will all be wondering about the absolutely life and death messages you might be missing, but guess what? When you turn the gadgets back on, just like magic the messages will appear...so nobody will be missing anything—just putting it on hold for a time.

An obvious but often overlooked family time takes place at the dinner table. While schedules can be crazy and overloaded, there will be plenty of times when most if not all of your family is home for supper. Sit at the table and shut off the television. Electronic gadgets need to be left elsewhere to eliminate outside interruptions. Dinner time still proves to be the most overlooked bonding time of the day, when kids share the stories of their day and families are able to laugh, and bond.

Something we do around our dinner table is ask the question, "What was the best and worst parts of your day?" Without exception, we hear one big universal grunt because nobody ever wants to answer the question. Also without exception, the answers reveal interesting things about their days and we end up having interesting conversations about them. It causes everyone to think back on their day and share experiences—both good and bad—with those who love them.

We have a devotional book at the table and after every supper meal one of the kids reads the day's devotional. It takes only a few minutes, but the conversation which follows always reveals personal thoughts often opening the door to instil Godly values and wisdom into their lives.

## Create a Weekly Family Night

Once a week, purposefully set aside an evening to spend together. Pick a night (the same night each week works well and avoids confusion) and plan something fun. Look at it as if you are having a date night with your kids. This is not the evening to have friends over because it's all about the family unit. People act differently when others are around, even if they think they don't.

It is important to limit family night to just your own family because the kids need to know that they are special and fun. Plus, you want to be selfish and have them all to yourself just for a little while. Don't fear, this doesn't need to be four or five hours' worth of fun. An hour or two is a good timeframe to plan for.

Age appropriateness is a necessary ingredient on family night. This can be tricky if you have kids from different age categories and genders, but with some thought and effort, not only can it be accomplished, it will create an opportunity to learn the fine art of give and take.

After all electronic gadgets have been shut off, the dishes washed, and homework completed, gather together and intentionally enjoy one another. Whether a movie with popcorn, a board game, or (if you have all girls) a mani-pedi session in the living room, there are countless things you can do together.

At our own home, every Tuesday is family night. Often we will watch a movie with a thousand snacks, because we all enjoy movies (and snacks). But every once in a while, someone will dig out a favourite board game and we will gather around the dining room table, pour a couple bags of chips and some ice tea, and have fun with it. In fact, I'm constantly amazed by the fun that is had around that table. We giggle and laugh and tell jokes.

While the kids may have started the game angry because they had to leave their phone in their room, or wanted to play something else or not play at all, within minutes they have forgotten their gripes and are holding their stomachs laughing. In fact, quite often when the game is finished and the snacks have been devoured, someone will dig out the cards and we will go right on playing games. What started out as a "have to" quickly turns into a "want to."

It is not a difficult idea, nor does it take much effort. But it does take discipline and commitment. It means learning to value that time so deeply that you say no to other things. Eventually your children will grow to value it as well. Before you know it, they will be reminding you that "tonight's family night" and will be eagerly anticipating it.

While the options for activities may be wide open, ensure that everyone gets a voice and it does not become a "have to do," but a "want to do." Have everyone take turns planning the evening. It only needs to be a couple of hours, but those couple of hours will become memory-building times for your entire family. Not everyone might enjoy playing a board game, but if little Suzie plans an evening of games with nachos and cheese, darling Billy will have to simply respect his little sister enough to enjoy her interests, because next week will be his turn and not likely everyone will enjoy his plans (specifically Suzie).

It is a teaching opportunity to allow our children to learn to respect others and be thoughtful, not self-centered. If everyone's interests are met on a regular basis, it won't be so difficult to participate in sister's activity if brother knows his turn is next.

## Make Your Home Welcoming

Learn to be the kind of parent who is not an embarrassment to your kids. Now, half the fun of being a parent is the ability to embarrass our children. As much fun as this is, save it for times when it won't disable the relationship either with your children or their friends, or both.

Kids should want to have their friends over, and if they don't we need to take a serious look at the reasons for this desired avoidance. One great way to determine why our kids may not want to bring their friends over is to ask them. Kids will be open and honest if we allow them to have a voice. Make sure your child knows you are asking because you honestly want to know what you can change or do differently so they will want to bring their friends over with confidence.

If you immediately start to defend yourself or make excuses, you might as well kiss honest communication goodbye. Your child will quickly learn that you are not interested in creating a safe (embarrassment-free) zone for them and their friends.

Our homes need to be that safe place for our kids—and their friends. Now, I can hear you screeching, "Are you kidding me? I want my kids to go to their friends' houses so that I can have some peace and quiet at home for a while." While I understand this desire, it is a selfish one.

I am quite aware that us moms get very little time for the needed and desired "peace and quiet." However, moms, we will get our peace and quiet in due time. There will come a day when our child trades in the comfort of our nest for college, a job, or a spouse of their own, and you will long for that hustle and bustle of squeals and giggles that will never again be heard. (Yes, you will one day actually miss that sound).

Make your home the one that is the gathering place for your child or teenager and their friends. Believe me, you would rather have them at your house knowing what they are up to then at someone else's house where you have no idea what they are doing, who they are with, what they are watching or whom they are listening to. Invest the time now and it will pay off in the future—both for you and your children.

## Traditions

A tradition is an activity of some type, whether big or small, free or expensive, that a family participates in to distinguish their family unit from other family units. Traditions can be daily (such as saying grace before the meal), weekly (such as family night), monthly, or even yearly (like decorating the Christmas tree).

Every family should have some traditions that are steeped in biblical fashion. However, traditions need no specific root, ancestry, or heritage. Although many traditions have been passed from generation to generation, we can create new traditions that are unique only to our family.

It is very important to have traditions, whether they are a hundred years old, passed down from great granny Jones, or brand new ones that you have created yourself for your own household. In fact, both are equally important and need to be implemented into our homes on a regular basis, and even more so into single parent homes. Traditions are like the glue that helps hold families together and impacts every member of the family unit in numerous ways, leaving a life-long mark on the heart.

Traditions give both children and teenagers a sense of family and security which is something we all need more of, especially when the family has broken down and our precious children's sense of security has been shaken. While some things may be changing, ensuring that some things stay the same will re-establish a foundation for that necessary sense of structure and stability.

Traditions also tend to foster closeness both in our immediate and extended families. Traditions form lasting memories and our children will carry at least some of these memorable traditions into their own homes as they become adults and have families of their own.

I've heard it said that traditions are the "we always" of families, like "We always make snow drinks at the first snowfall," or "We always watch a new release movie and eat popcorn on Tuesday night." Because such traditions have meaning that is special to an individual family, they create feelings of warmth and closeness. By spending time together in comfortable, fun and special settings, family members create a bond of closeness and unity which will be difficult to break, regardless of the circumstances that may come our way.

Effective traditions promote a sense of identity and a feeling of belonging. They also promote a feeling of safety and security within the family by providing a predictable and familiar experience. Family members have something to look forward to which gives them a sense of assurance in a hectic and ever-changing world. When our kids grow up and leave the nest for a life of their own, it is the traditions that will bring them—and their own families—back home.

Family bonds can be weakened by over involved and busy lifestyles, but families can remain connected by intentionally maintaining important and valuable family traditions. Traditions, such as family night, must be intentional or they will quickly fade out and the memories will be lost.

I would guess that before you were a single parent, you had some family traditions. If you were married, your husband's family perhaps had some traditions, too, and I'm going to guess that you implemented some of each into your family unit. Once you had children, they too learned to enjoy those traditions. Now that you are a single parent, you might be tempted to neglect those traditions that originated with your ex-partner. With all your might, resist this temptation and do not throw away half of your traditions. Remember, they are also your children's traditions.

Of course, you should come up with some of your own and begin having fun in your newly revised family unit again. I recall the first Christmas my sons were to go to their father's for the holiday. I battled for weeks over just how to handle it. "Do I give them their gifts before or after? I'd like to experience a nice Christmas dinner together, but they won't be here."

Finally, after praying and asking God for wisdom on how best to handle this new "tradition" of having to spend every other Christmas without my sons, and sons who must now spend every other Christmas without their mom, I implemented my own tradition which is unique to my own family.

The evening before they go to their father's for Christmas, I cook everyone's favourite things for one big meal. It is not your usual Christmas dinner (mostly because I can't cook a turkey), because it is everyone's favourite dishes. One son loves shrimp and baked Brie while another enjoys chicken wings and perogies. It is a very unusual meal, but it has become our every-other-Christmas tradition.

While I set the table up with a holly-printed tablecloth, candles, steamy hot food, and Christmas crackers, the boys are getting dressed because, after all, it's a fancy dinner so we must look fancy. We all come together in our fancy clothes, freshly combed hair, and huge appetites, spending hours around the overindulgent table. It is similar to a festival, with the numerous courses, the fancy cider with cinnamon sticks, shiny Christmas crackers, tissue paper crowns and such.

After the food has been devoured and we are all so full we can hardly get off the chairs, we move to the living room where I turn on the Christmas tree lights, refill the apple cider mugs, and hand each one of my boys a handmade personal gift bag. This is a precursor to their actual Christmas gifts, but the joy they experience and the brilliant smiles that flash across their faces bring as much joy as any Christmas morning ever has.

These personalized, hand-painted bags are filled with all their favourite things: items they have seen at the store and pointed out months earlier, favourite candies, and some items that are unique just to them, such as a fishing rod lighter for my son who is a fishing fanatic.

It is so much fun and is one tradition that was started because of the change that was brought on from our family breakdown. Good things can come from bad experiences if we put forth the effort and ask God for His divine wisdom. Rather than mope around and feel sorry for ourselves, we need to raise our heads up and turn the bad into good, with Christ's help.

We have created numerous traditions in our home, from these big once a year day-long festivities to small, quick daily traditions. My youngest son and I have played a bedtime game since he was four years old. One warm summer night, while visiting my parents and I had just put my darling son to bed, we had a quick little moment where he said "I love you" and I responded with "I love you more" and walked out of the room.

A few moments later, I spewed hot coffee all over the kitchen table—and my mother—as we heard a little voice holler from the end of the hallway. "I love *you* more." I walked toward the little voice while wiping coffee off myself and peeked into his room. I laid down beside my son and whispered, "I love you more." This game went on for quite some time and he was doing a very good job of keeping me right there in his room—which is probably the game he was really playing.

After a while, I leaned over and whispered, "I love you more so live with it." He was nearly asleep by this time, so he just grinned and fell asleep. He is thirteen now, but ever since that night nine years ago, there are very few nights that pass where one of us doesn't blurt out "I love you more so live with it" as he goes to bed. Even on the nights when he is not sleeping at my house, whether he is at his father's, his grandmother's or a friend's for the night, one of us will send a text around the time he goes to bed saying the peaceful statement.

I have often made him a little note if he is not going to see me before bed with the saying doodled on it and he has one note taped to his bedroom wall. It is a daily simple tradition, but one that says, "Hey, everything is okay today, and by the way, I love you."

You see, traditions don't need to be expensive or difficult or time-consuming; they do need to be fun and meaningful and something that is bonding to the family unit. They give the message that "everything is okay" and "I am loved."

### Participate in Your Child's Life

If your family is anything like the rest of the world, you are busy...and your children are busier. In fact, busy is such an understatement. Yet here I come, suggesting that you add to your already over crowded schedule. Actually, what I am suggesting is that you slow down, take a step back from the business of life and enjoy your children and allow them to enjoy you.

Kids today have so many opportunities that sometimes I find my head spinning with all the things they do. There is soccer, basketball, hockey, piano, drumming, dance, this club, that group, and the list goes on and on and on. Add to this homework, school activities, friends and hopefully chores, and there is more activity than time. How can a mom possibly keep up with such craziness?

I won't tell you it is easy because I have a strong anti-lie policy and that would certainly be one erroneous lie. However, I will tell you it's possible, because I did it. When I was in college, I had three sons playing hockey. Between Monday and Sunday, practices and games, I found myself going to the hockey rink between nine and twelve times a week. I was getting frustrated and would stay up till the wee hours of the morning (after the little hockey stars were fed, showered, and safely tucked into their beds) doing homework, reading textbooks, and getting prepared for the next day's classes.

I noticed that my sons started to feel bad about my situation and it turns out I was giving off a "your activities are a bother to me" vibe. I knew that would end badly, so I went to the Lord and asked for wisdom. I had to somehow learn to enjoy living at the hockey rink, but I also needed to have my school work done. I needed something only He could give me—a plan.

Turns out, homework can be done at the hockey rink. I ended up doing the majority of my winter semester's work at the rink. I was the only mom who attended every game that year, as well as a number of practices. I often looked like a fool, but it was comforting for my boys to look up into the stands and see me there. My sons have since shared with me what that meant to them and how it allowed them to feel important and valued. I ended up graduating a semester early, so just following God's path I earned my degree *and* gave my sons an invaluable gift.

Your situation may be different. In fact, I'm quite sure it is. What is the same, however, is a desire for a great outcome for our children. I am sure you, too, want to empower your children with the gift of importance and value. If you ask the Lord to give you wisdom, He will do so. He knows your specific circumstances, financial situation, time schedule, and personal desires better than anyone else. He will show you specific ways—if you are willing—to give your children the gift of time and value.

So many young people today are saying, "My parents never came to my games," "They never saw me throw the winning basket," or "They never saw me trip and make a fool of myself." Our noticeable absence discourages our kids and gives them a feeling of being unimportant and worthless. Moms, we need to make our children's activities a priority in our lives—putting them ahead of our own tasks, if necessary.

There are so many ways to fit family time into our days, but we must be willing to do so. Before we will be willing to put forth that effort, we need to intrinsically understand the high importance of doing so. I guarantee that, when you make it a priority and start implementing family time into your routine, you will begin to notice a radical change in your child's spirits and sense of personal value, which will in turn create positive changes in their attitudes and behaviours.

Your family will begin enjoying one another and looking forward to those special times and it will be fun. Families absolutely must have fun on a regular basis in order to have a reason (rather than an obligation) to build unity and a strong familial structure.

Moms, if you will put forth the effort by facilitating and encouraging family times, family traditions, and opportunities for your kids' friends to be comfortable in your home, you will quickly begin to notice positive changes in your family unit. Your kids will begin to feel valued and respected, and in turn they will start to value and respect you. They will begin to notice that they matter to you, and you will begin to sincerely matter to them. Once you instil value into any person, whether grandma, the next door neighbour or your children, that person cannot help but respond to you—and to life—from a place of value.

If our words speak, then surely our actions will scream. When we begin to value our children by our actions, our children will begin to act from a place of value, rather than a place of anger, hurt, or resentment. Try it, then sit back and enjoy the positive, life-changing transformation.

# DATING WITH KIDS

For reasons I cannot determine, a majority of women—especially those of us with children—believe to a large extent that we are incomplete on our own; we need a man to make us a whole person. Our "other half," as we refer to him. Recently, I had a mom of three kids, frantic and teary, stop by my office. Her kids are not babies; they are all into their teens. Her children are respectful, thoughtful, and very caring. They absolutely love their mom and she is, for the most part, an excellent mother.

Unfortunately, this lady's first husband was a demanding, controlling, violent man. He was abusive in every possible way towards his wife, and after threatening her life, she had the police escort him out and was able to get a substantial restraining order on him. This order only referred to her, though, and not the children. This man had never been abusive in any way to the children, and therefore his visitation and access agreement remained intact.

You would hope that one would learn a lifelong valuable lesson from such horrific experiences but rather than carry these lessons into our later lives, we unfortunately find ourselves right back in similar situations over and over.

After nearly ten years of being on her own, raising wonderful children, and doing some great things with her life, she remarried a man who promised to love her and look after her and do all the things a great husband is supposed to do. He didn't do any of those things. Rather, he chose to threaten her life, and attempt to ruin her children.

She sat down and began to unload her burden. I listened with compassion and frustration. This lady said over and over again, "I deserve a family. Why can't I have a family? I just want a family." I looked at her with what I'm sure she thought was disdain. It wasn't. It was complete confusion.

I asked what her idea of family was and she quickly rambled off her thoughts. I had to absolutely disagree with her and pointed out that she did have a family. A wonderful family, at that. She had a beautiful home with family pictures covering her walls. She had all the things you need when you have a family: comfortable furniture, cupboards full of dishes, beds, an overburdened shoe rack, a crazy schedule filled with dance and hockey and soccer and school events and meetings.

When did we decide that we are not a family if there is no adult male posing in our family photos? What makes us think that we cannot be happy unless there is a man to say "Thanks for supper," or "Have you seen my car keys?"

I reiterated numerous times to this mom that she was indeed part of a magnificent family, but she did not—or would not—hear me. She was believing the lie that so many of us women fall into—we are incomplete without a man.

Recently, I was in church and one of our grade twelve graduates wore her graduation dress so we could all "ooooh" and "ahhhh" over it. It was definitely gorgeous, light green in color, with a sheer lace overlay and delicate dark green embroidered stitching across the sleeveless bodice. It made me want to go home and pull out my old high school graduation gown and relive the memories (if only I could remember that far back).

Of course, I wouldn't do such a thing, because someone would inevitably squeal, "Try it on…try it on," and of course I would try desperately to pull the long zipper up to the top all the while muttering, "I'm sure it still fits," sucking in everything I possibly could suck in, adjusting and readjusting the boobs and pulling the delicate cloth every which way, all in a feeble attempt to get that zipper up. (Yes, this entire scene horrifically played out in my mind as I gazed at this poor girl).

I was jolted back to reality and literally at a loss for words when one of the older ladies at the church said to this beauty in the green dress, "Now if only you had a nicely dressed young man to stand beside you, this picture would be complete." I was horrified! *Horrified*!

No one has yet been able to tell me for certain which garden grew this ridiculous notion. It is not a beautiful flower but more like a prickly, poisonous weed that needs to be ripped out at the roots and quickly discarded. Insecticide, pesticide, stupidicide or ridiculous-cide; whatever 'cides' we need to get rid of this horrific weed, then pull it out, turn up nozzle to full blast, and shoot away.

Perhaps many decades before this one, before women were allowed to be educated or have a paying job, before social assistance or student loans, a woman—especially a mother— needed a man. It was mandatory for survival. However, let me remind you that it was for financial and familial reasons, not for self-worth or to be "complete." This is no longer the case and women can—and do—make life work very well on their own.

## But I Want a Partner

It would be nice to have a man around to take out the trash or unclog the sink. Of course, us women don't mind being pampered or romanced. Having our car started or the oil checked would be great. Cuddling on the sofa watching a late night romantic flick by candle light would be acceptable.

Realistically, we know that along with these wonderful positives also come numerous negatives. Some are acceptable and some are not. I am certainly not a man hater, nor am I bashing any of the male species, so please don't read into this that I am. I am remarried to a wonderful man, but let me assure you (and my husband would certainly concur), remarriage can be hard.

Of course, the majority of individuals still desire a life-long partner, but there is an enormous difference between "want" and "need." The Lord says He will meet all of our needs, not necessarily our wants, and we must learn to trust Him in His word and believe that He knows what is best for us at all times.

When my teenager wants to date someone who is not good for them and will drag them down or be a negative influence in their life, I let him know that he needs to make a choice. Either date someone who is a healthy, positive individual or don't date. It's just that simple, yet it's excruciatingly difficult. So it is with us, but on a much grander scale.

When we were teenagers and young adults, dating was a roller coaster ride. Can you recall? It was a cycle of ups and downs with your stomach in your throat most of the time. Good or bad, joy or pain, dating was vicious. Personally, my biggest worry as a dating teenager was over exactly when my mother would start flicking the porch lights, indicating that she could see us through the living room window and had not one, but two eyes firmly planted on our every movement lest we get within three feet of each other.

If I thought that was horrible, I would have traded my mom's two prying eyes for my children's six watchful glaring eyes any day. They watched me ever more intently, wondering if they still held priority, if they were still important.

Once we have children attached to us, dating becomes nearly impossible. As moms, our time is valuable and our children precious. Dating as a mom involves a balancing act that even the most seasoned circus performer would fail to manoeuvre. There are no classes to take, no schedules to use, and no maps to follow.

We need to internalize the truth that we are wonderful and fulfilled and fully complete without a man to barbeque the burgers, tie the skates, or open the pickle jar (they have come up with fancy gadgets for these things now). If the Lord brings a man into our life who meets our standards, we can consider ourselves deeply blessed.

It is when we get discouraged and lonely that we begin heading to the internet or the coffee shop or the Laundromat (even when we own our own washer and dryer) in desperate attempts to "find a man." I am sure we've all been there. I had a season pass! Good heavens, I used to go to the mall just to smell a man's cologne as he walked past. Good grief, how silly that seems but it just goes to show how crazy we can let ourselves become when we fall into the trap of loneliness.

## First Things First

We need to learn to enjoy ourselves and our freedoms, being secure in who we are, and learn the difference between being alone and being lonely. Unless we become secure in our own skin, no man will ever complete us or fill our lonely hearts. We must learn to be satisfied and fully complete with ourselves and the Lord. It is only then, that we can find satisfaction and joy in a relationship. It is only then that we can give ourselves completely to anyone without walls or false expectations or cracked self-images.

Two incomplete people can never make two complete people. However, two complete, healthy, whole individuals does equal more joy and contentment than one has ever desired. Before we have dealt with our own rubbish, laid it down, walked away, and found our identity in Christ, we have absolutely no place in the dating world.

We all need to do ourselves an enormous favour and learn the difference between being alone and being lonely. We can be in a crowd of a million people and have a lonely heart. We can come from a large family, with brothers and sisters on every street, and feel lonely. We can be in a marriage and suffer from loneliness.

When we have Christ in the very center of our lives we will not struggle with loneliness, because Christ is our forever friend. He will never leave us and His Word says that He is a friend who sticks closer than a brother. So, we need never be lonely.

We can, however, be alone, and that is not a bad thing. Everyone needs some time alone in order to hear the voice of the Lord and meditate on His Word. It is impossible to be alone in a crowd. On the other hand, crowds are absolutely overflowing with lonely people.

Now that we know the difference between being lonely and being alone, we can understand that a man, a mate, a partner, a spouse, will not change a lonely heart—only God can do that. If we have Christ, we are never lonely.

If we are wanting a man to be a part of our lives, then we must make absolutely sure that it is for the right reasons and that you are not "looking" for a partner. I know of an individual who was separated from his spouse, yet still legally married to her. They had been separated for a couple of years with no intention of hurrying a divorce along. While the husband wanted the divorce, his wife did not and chose to drag it out for as long as she had the power to do so. This husband decided that he was moving on regardless and soon began dating.

Before long, he found a woman he was very interested in and within a very short time had proposed to her. She readily accepted, assuming he was divorced, and he did not tell her otherwise. They set a date, made the preparations, sent out the invitations, and had everything ready to go—except the divorce certificate.

Two weeks before the wedding date, this husband was getting desperate. He had begged and pleaded his wife to sign the divorce papers, yet she refused. At the end of his rope, he made some very damaging threats against his wife, using the children as pawns. It worked and his wife signed the papers; he was now free to marry his next wife.

They are still together, and the second wife has no idea that she was engaged to a married man. The hard fast rule should always be, "Without a legalized divorce certificate (and not just one in the process), or you are not married, *do not date*." Its quite simple, really. By adamantly following this very simple rule, you will save yourself, your children, and the future love of your life a lot of grief and pain.

God knows your heart and says that He will give you the desires of your heart. Knowing God's promise then, begin praying for him to cross your path in God's time and not yours. The Lord knows who you need and who will be a positive person for your children. He will bring that particular individual to you at just the right moment.

I frequently have people ask me to pray that their children find good friends. We often pray that prayer for our children when they head off to that first day of school or youth group, because we know that friends are a very influential part of our children's lives. If we can pray with confidence that the Lord will bring solid, positive friends along for our children, we certainly should be able to have that same faith for God to bring a solid, positive man into our lives. While you are praying for such a man (and yes, ladies, the world is full of great Godly men), begin to be proactive in preparing your life for a partner.

## God the Matchmaker

Proverbs 14:1 tells us that a *"wise woman builds her house, but with her own hands, the foolish one tears hers down."* I believe you very wise women need to begin thinking about what type of man a wise woman might want.

Literally get out a pen and a notepad and make a very specific list. This list should be multifaceted. Part A needs to include those things that you personally desire in a man and a relationship. Include everything you can think of that you would really find necessary. My list included things like:

1. He must have children of his own.
2. He must love the Lord with all his heart.
3. He must have a compassionate heart.
4. He must be healthy, but not a fitness/gym addict.
5. He must have a sense of humour.
6. He must be able to laugh at himself.
7. He must be able to apologize.
8. He must be at least six feet tall.

Of course this is not my complete list, as that would take pages. I was very specific, and so should you be. God has given us each likes and dislikes. He has blessed us with different desires and passions. Some of you may be very much into fitness and have a lifetime membership to the gym, and that is wonderful. You would desire someone who was also equally passionate about fitness so that you could participate in such activities together. On the other hand, some of you may think that spending so much time at a gym, or on fitness in general, to be selfish and prideful, so being in a relationship with someone like that would become difficult for you both.

Someone once told me that these lists are very selfish and that we should be happy with whomever we find. I strongly disagree, because this hopefully is a life-long relationship and we obviously want it to be as strong as possible. That means we have to be very choosy. It is perfectly fine to settle on a puppy or a hamster or a home or a book. Those things, while important, will not have the capacity to make our lives—and our children's lives—miserable. People have that ability so we absolutely cannot settle in this area.

Part B of this list is the very opposite of part A. Part B are those quirks or characteristics that you absolutely will not tolerate in a relationship. While it might seem redundant to literally get out a pen and write these things down, it is absolutely necessary. By doing this we give thought to what we normally do not think about.

We must proactively consider what is simply not acceptable to us. If we fail to do so, we will quickly find ourselves in a situation where there is a man interested in us whose company we enjoy and who treats us quite well, though he does certain things that bother us immensely. Cursing in traffic, for example. Or being unable to manage his feelings appropriately, thus having angry outbursts at you or your children.

I can hear you saying, "If that happened, I would break that relationship off," and I know that we all think that way. We tend to give ourselves more credit before the situation arises than we do when we are in the middle of it. We battle with our minds, saying "Well, he treats me so well most of the time. I can overlook his angry outbursts once in a while." These are the exact areas where you will later find yourself saying angrily, "What have I done? Why didn't I see this before?" when in fact you did, and chose to overlook it.

The Part B list is crucial. People do not often change just because a ceremony takes place. Those annoying characteristics that you thought you could change, or you thought wouldn't bother you, will be magnified a hundred fold. Decide, when there is no emotional risk, what you will not tolerate in a relationship. Again, here are a few samples of my own list:

1. I will not tolerate road rage.
2. I will not tolerate lying.
3. I will not tolerate cutting remarks to my children.
4. I will not tolerate controlling behaviour.

If we don't make a list, we are setting ourselves up to be caught in a trap. We may find someone who has numerous characteristics from Part A, date him for a number of months, fall in love, and become engaged. Our hearts will get so entangled that our minds will not be heard. We've all had the battles between our hearts and our minds; the result from those battles are not usually simple or clear-cut. If we have made lists of these things before our hearts get enmeshed or our minds become fuzzy with emotion, it will be much clearer when we need to make lifelong decisions that will change our lives forever.

The Lord Himself instructs us to *"wait for the Lord; be strong and take heart and wait for the Lord"* (Psalm 27:14). He has a perfect mate for us, and if we stop searching long enough for the Lord to work, He will bring that lifelong partner right to us. When the time is right, God will put your perfect match smack dab in the middle of your path for you to trip over—just watch and see!

## I Found Mr. Right... Now What?

Once God has placed someone in your path with whom you believe you could have a lasting relationship, hundreds of questions will require answers. "Do I tell my kids that I'm going on a date? How do I tell them? What if they react poorly? What do I wear? How much personal information do I share with this man on a first date?" The questions are endless and there are no sure answers. (That's reassuring, isn't it?) The answers will very much depend on your situation and family. You know your children better than anyone else, so you will have to carefully monitor the situation and respond accordingly.

While there is no one answer that will work for every situation, there are some general guidelines that we can discuss. Implementing them into your own situation will surely save you and your children much heartache, doubt, and anxiety—things we all like to avoid.

Before you jump into any relationship, speak to your children on a general basis and get their feelings and input into your possible dating life. If we are proactive with this, we will be able to steer clear of potential issues later on. If we talk openly with our children before we are dating, we will be able to hear them clearly without feeling attacked or needing to justify a situation we may already find ourselves in.

It is vital that our children know their opinions matter and that we deeply value their input into our lives. My own sons were so protective of me that if a man even pretended to look my way, he was in for a sad awakening. We were in the dentist's office one afternoon when a man across the waiting room was very obviously staring in my direction. My oldest son noticed this long before I did and started to become very fidgety. He kept wanting to leave the building, but I thought it was because he didn't want to see the dentist.

Trying to calm him down, I noticed that his fists were beginning to turn white and realized that he was quickly becoming angry. I thought we could take a short walk outside so he could calm down and tell me what was going on. As I stood up, I noticed the man staring. (Ladies, you know what I mean when I say my "creep" sense immediately kicked in). I went to the desk and rebooked our appointments and quickly left the building.

I could have gotten upset with my son, but that would not have done any good and it certainly would not have sent my son the right message. He was the oldest and for some reason had a belief that it was up to him to protect me. In his mind, he was only doing what a young man was supposed to do. This led to a conversation about dating which was very enlightening.

Kids generally believe—or want to believe—that mommy and daddy are going to magically forget and forgive, miraculously come to their senses, and get back together. I learned that day that to moms, dating means moving on; to her children, mom dating means the end of a fantasy. It means mom and dad are not getting back together and it means they must accept the breakdown of their family.

When you have this conversation with your children, be lovingly honest. Relate to the children at their age level and never give them a false hope of their family reuniting if you know for certain it will not happen. Let them experience whatever emotions they need to feel: anger, tears, or frustration. It is important that you allow them the safety to feel all the ugliness of what your truthful discussion will bring.

It won't last forever, but they have a right to their feelings. If they do not feel safe sharing them, they will stuff them. You will see little bits and pieces of these emotions peek out once in a while, but your children will never be able to come to grips with their emotions and release them in a healthy manner. You probably will not like this and may become frustrated. But just hold on, mom, with security and love; it will not last long.

Now that you have had this initial conversation, be patient and wait until your children have come to terms with it before you rush right out on a man hunt. If you have some wonderful man knocking on your door, it is okay to let him know that you need a bit of time to let your children settle into the idea of mom dating before you actually do anything about it. If he is the kind of man that you need in your life, he will graciously give you the time and space you need. If he becomes demanding and impatient, that is a great indication he is not the one for you and move on (meaning, quickly run away).

Okay. Your children have settled into the idea and are somewhat comfortable—or learning to be comfortable—with the idea and you are feeling it is safe to take that next step. It is not wise to bring home every man that looks in your direction. While there may be plenty of fish in the sea, we do not need to have them all swim over to our supper table. We definitely want the kids to be involved for a variety of reasons, but if you develop a pattern of dating numerous men, the kids will become attached to at least some of them. Remember that your children have already gone through a loss with the breakdown of their family, so they don't need to go through anymore. Protect them from this.

It is difficult for children to spend time and become attached to mom's boyfriend only to see the relationship break up and watch him leave. Our kids attach to men in a very different way than us women do. If this happens too often, the children will become detached from men in general and when you do find the one whom you want to spend your life with, the children will have developed a "Yeah right, he'll be gone next week just like the others" attitude and attachments will become difficult and unstable.

Ladies, be wise. We can have a plethora of friends, both male and female, and that's okay. Keep a careful eye on your children's reactions and adjust your social life accordingly. If they are starting to whine that you are always out or not home or don't have time for them, pull back and love on your kids. Don't get angry or frustrated with them, or they will start wondering if they are just getting in the way of your social life.

## Find a Balance

Finding a balance that works for everyone is nearly impossible, but at least give it your best effort. If Mr. Right has children of his own, that balance is going to be even more difficult to find. But it's out there somewhere—search for it. Communication is an absolute asset between you, Mr. Right, and your children. When one or more of the children start having questions, answer them honestly.

If you watch carefully, you will be able to monitor your children's attitudes and help them along in the process. Balance is the key. It is a wise mom who knows when to show affection and when to save it for another time. Kids watch. It's like they have a hundred eyes that see all things. Make wise and thoughtful choices.

Remember that you are wonderful and excellent and worthwhile and complete and valuable. No man is going to complete you, because the only one who has the ability to do that is Christ alone. Be complete in Him and, if the day comes, He will bring just the right man into your life; you and your children will be blessed.

# POSITIVE CO-PARENTING

Positive co-parenting…what an oxymoron. I can hear you now, shrieking at the top of your lungs, *"Are you kidding me?"* No. I am not kidding at all. It is possible.

While experiencing the breakdown of one's family is tragic and emotionally overpowering, there are always strategies we can implement into the situation to make it just a bit less catastrophic for our children. After all, they are the ones who take the brunt of all the emotional chaos. They get mom's emotions, they get dad's emotions, and woven in amongst that roller coaster of a mess are their own emotions, which they must somehow decipher and deal with.

When we and our partner go separate ways, we are not always saddened. Often the family breakdown is pre-empted by numerous incidents such as vicious or continual arguing. There may have been excessive drinking, sexual affairs (or emotional ones), or addictions of various sorts. Or perhaps you simply just "fell out of love" and moved on.

Whatever the reason, you may have been relieved to find some peace from the situation. Perhaps it was you who left the relationship. Maybe you were the one who was left, and you spent several months in complete heartbreak. Either way, your children are stuck trying to miraculously figure out these feelings that they likely have never experienced before and are not naturally equipped to handle.

Regardless of the circumstances which end the relationship, the cold hard truth is that is has ended. Because we are female and because we are emotional beings, we likely had a meltdown of one sort or another when we found ourselves parenting alone. We may have thrown a party, which throws our children into chaos and brings a whole new set of feelings and emotions and questions, or we laid on the couch depressed and rejected. Either way, we faced emotional overload.

Furthermore, we likely (unknowingly) put some of our emotional distress onto our children. No matter how we may have tried to hide our emotions, our children felt them. I have talked to people who "sat the kids down and laid it out for them because they just needed to know the truth about the other parent." Sadly, that truth was by perception only and not what the kids needed to hear.

There is a concrete rule of thumb which we can count on when it comes to being a single parent and co-parenting: if you would be upset by your ex-partner telling your children something about you, then don't tell your children something about him. Remember, kids love both parents and want a relationship with both of them.

It is the parent who attempts to sabotage the children's relationship with the other parent who ends up losing. The children may stay quiet for the time being, but they are internalizing who is saying what about whom. When they are grown and find their voice, they will certainly use it and you might not like what they have to say.

It is always about the kids—never about us. It is always in their best interest to speak positively about their father and co-parent in a manner that reflects the love for your children rather than your personal hurts and demands for justice. Your children will respect you for it.

## What the Children Need

I have spent years talking to young people of all ages about their personal experiences of living in split homes. Sadly, the vast majority of them say the same things. They have very similar complaints and concerns.

Many of the kids I talk to don't necessarily mind their parents' divorces or separations and have learned to adjust to their circumstances. They enjoy the peace that comes from their parents not hollering and yelling at one another anymore. Children often find that their parents are both much happier when they are not together. Kids can come up with numerous positives about their situation. They don't love going back and forth between two homes, but they adjust because they love their parents.

What they do mind (hate is usually the word they squeeze out from between gritted teeth) is being put in the middle. They detest hearing parents say mean and hurtful things about one another and they absolutely abhor not having a voice and not being heard.

Our children suffer emotionally when we slash at their fathers. He is part of our children and we can never change that. When we disrespect him, we disrespect them. How we may feel about our children's father is absolutely irrelevant, but often the kids internalize those feelings and take them upon themselves. "If mom hates dad and I look just like dad, she must hate me too." I know that none of us particularly want to believe that. Nonetheless, truth is truth, whether we believe it or not.

However we want to justify our actions or our words, it is still wrong and feels like daggers hitting straight into our children's spirits. None of us want to harm our children, so we must put down our weapons of warfare and pick up the armour of God's love, forgiveness, and peace. We do not need to love our ex-partners, but we absolutely must love and respect our children enough to put down our weapons.

## No More Excuses

Whenever I encourage moms to strive towards being a healthy co-parent, I usually get the same response. "Well, you obviously do not know my child's father. There is absolutely no way to get along with that man for even five minutes. If you only knew what I go through, you would never even suggest such a thing." (I could list hundreds more, several which came from my own mouth, but you get my point).

Oh yes, I have heard it all and lived a lot of it. My children's father and I wished each other dead for a number of years (don't worry ladies, this is normal) and we often verbalized such things in numerous loud arguments we've had over the years.

Now, it shouldn't be implied that just because you make a choice to be a great co-parent, your ex-partner will do likewise. Nor does it suggest that you must move into some odd, flourishing friendship with your ex-partner. It simply means that we must put our children's best interests before our own hurts and resentments.

Please understand that co-parenting is not always a possibility. There are hundreds of fathers in prisons all over North America. Even more have simply walked away and want nothing to do with you or their children. Some of you have experienced such severe abuses that restraining orders have been granted and it would be unsafe to have your children around such a person.

These are not excuses, but valid reasons. We must always protect our children to the very best of our abilities. Not agreeing with some of the parenting styles our ex-partner might use, however, is not a reason; it is an excuse.

Moms, emotionally supporting our kids means keeping our hurts to ourselves. So many young people tell me that they don't want to be their parents' sounding boards. They never asked to be the messengers and they certainly feel belittled and bullied when they must listen to cut downs and disrespectful comments about one parent from the other.

While we should not vent to our children, it is very important that we do have a strong sounding board. We are certainly allowed to vent and scream and holler when situations arise with our ex-partner. That is why we have friends. One of the most detrimental issues for our kids is to have them as our sounding boards or confidantes. They are not emotionally able to handle such hurtful weight. Children should never be required to comfort their parents' hurts. When we behave in such a way that our children are compelled to comfort us, it damages them long-term.

We must set aside all of our excuses and realize that there are areas we can make changes in. Then we must implement those changes. Regardless of how well we may have co-parented in the past, we can all do a better job in the future. If we want to know where we are failing in this area and where we can step it up, we can ask our children. They are very helpful in their opinions, because they are the ones experiencing it.

If you ask them where you can improve, listen to them and accept what they say. The moment you begin justifying your own actions, words, or behaviours is the exact moment when they will decide never to be caught in that trap again.

## He Won't Co-operate

Most often, only one parent in the co-parenting equation makes the effort. Usually, only one parent chooses to lay aside their hurts and resentments and desires for revenge and decides that their children's best interest take priority to their own anger and pride. You need to be that parent. If the other sees a change in you and decides to join you in the co-parenting journey, your children will be doubly blessed.

There are no guarantees, however, that this will happen. But, for your children's sake you must choose to lay down your own personal issues with their father and let him off the hook. It is only when you forgive him (and possibly his family), and allow yourself to see him as your children's father rather than the man who wounded you, that you will be able to step into a healthy co-parenting role.

The Lord encourages us to show mercy and be peacemakers. *"Blessed are the merciful, for they will be shown mercy. Blessed are the pure in heart, for they will see God. Blessed are the peacemakers, for they will be called [daughters] of God"* (Matthew 5:7-9).

### Reflecting a Heavenly Father

Being a peacemaker is tragically difficult most of the time, especially when we are asked to bring peace to an unpeaceful situation. Being a peacemaker often requires us to die to ourselves and our own desires in order to let peace inhabit the situation.

Again, I cannot say this enough—*always think of your children first.* I often hear moms say that they wish the guy would just disappear or maybe someone would just take him out and shoot him. While this brings a chuckle to our lips, we are not considering the needs of our children. I have said it and I can guess that you have, too.

Why would we say such things? Because it would make life easier for us. We may believe it would make life easier for our children if dad would simply fall off the earth, but that is certainly not true.

The saddest of all stories are the ones where dads just leave. No birthday cards or phone calls or Christmas presents. No "congratulations on your graduation" and no "hey, let's go to the ball game on Friday." We have believed for so long that this would be the easiest and the best, but it is simply untrue. Children suffer greatly when their father is not in their lives, at least to some extent. Do not be one to encourage his disappearance, because it will exponentially wound your child.

I have a very good friend whose father did just that. He just left. He didn't call or write or make any attempts to see his son. Every now and then, he'd show up in town and his son would see his truck or see him in a restaurant or the bank, but he never made the slightest of efforts to contact his son. The negative impact of this absentee father has damaged my friend to the core. He has grown into a man who admittedly trusts no one and certainly does not trust love or family bonds.

Even if our child's father is not what we think he should be, our children need a relationship with him. Make sure that it is never you who stands in the way of that relationship. Reflect the love and forgiveness of the Lord to your children by being a living example. Our kids need to see that we are adults and can get along reasonably well. There is never a need to have a screamfest at the front door every second Friday when daddy comes to pick up the kids. That is modeling selfishness and hatred—not what we want our children to see.

There are numerous ways we can encourage that relationship rather than stand in the way of it. If there is a ball game in town and your son happens to enjoy ball, send his father an email. It doesn't need to be long and drawn out. "I see there is a ball game on Friday night and I know you have season tickets. I know Justin was scheduled to be with me this weekend, but if you'd like to take him to the game, that would be great—he'd love to go." It's just that simple.

If you begin to encourage their relationship, you will find that it will be coming from the other direction as well. You will be getting the emails or texts offering kindness for the benefit of your children. There is only "mom's weekend" and "dad's weekend" in court papers and documents, but this is only necessary when adults fight over their children. Of course, at the beginning, this "time" schedule may be important in order to give everyone some stability in the situation but after a period of time this schedule should evaporate into thin air.

Stop for a moment and think of the pressure a child or teenager must feel when they don't really want to go to dad's for the weekend because there is a big event at their school on Saturday or a football game they wanted to be part of on Friday night. It must be terrible to have to give up their own wants and desires because they are obligated to be at one parent or the other's for that time. Let me state boldly, against much popular belief, that there is no "mom's time" and there is no "dad's time." All the time is the child's. It is their childhood. Parents and families must choose to stop fighting over that.

My children love me very much. I am very close with all three of my sons, who range in age from thirteen to nineteen years old. I do not demand time from them, nor does their father. We have allowed them to be in control of their own time.

I watch children all the time who must miss their volleyball tournament because it was their "weekend with mom." Maybe mom happens to live four or five hours away. If mom wants to be involved with her daughter, she needs to give up her time, make the drive, and be with her daughter. Somewhere along the line we have gotten our priorities mixed up and we absolutely must get them back before it is too late and we lose our children.

To their sobbing children who don't want to miss their friends sleepover on Saturday night, but must because it's dad's weekend, I have heard parents say, "We all need to make sacrifices in these situations." The unfortunate truth is that while sacrifices must be made, it is usually the children who make them.

I have heard very bold children shout at one parent or the other, "You and dad got divorced, but it's me who has to pay the price for it." They are exactly right. Moms, consider your children first.

## Practical Ways to Co-Parent

We have already mentioned a few ways to co-parent well. First, we must reshape our thinking. Our children are the priority. It is their childhood, so it is their time—not ours and not their fathers. If there are times when something is going on that your children want to attend with their father, let them attend and be happy about it.

Buy birthday gifts together. You do not necessarily need to go shopping together (that would be pushing it), but have a discussion about what your child would like to have for a birthday and one of you pick it up. Get the money first, if that will be an issue later, but get one card and both of you sign it. This might take some planning, especially if you live a good distance apart. It sounds difficult—it's really not if you set your mind to it.

Once we put down our stubbornness of being the victim or having to be right and let him off the hook for what we think he owes us, these things become relatively simple. The more you practice them, the easier they become, and the more blessed your children will be.

Another idea that works if you live relatively close, is to carve pumpkins together. Get together one evening with some apple cider or hot chocolate and a boxful of pumpkins. (Yes, I realize there are sharp objects in this plan that may be inappropriate, so use your judgement.) The kids will appreciate having the help of both mom and dad, and it will be a positive, long-lasting memory.

Take an evening and play a board game together. It is amazing how laughter can break the ice and mend past hurts. You certainly do not need to be friends outside of these infrequent events, but in front of the children you must put on your best happy face and enjoy yourself—and your children.

Go to a movie. You don't need to sit beside each other. In fact, kids are very smart and will most likely position themselves between you just to be sure there will be no fighting. I know these things sound absolutely absurd and ridiculous, and I am pretty sure you are rolling your eyes and mumbling that I am completely crazy. I am not just saying these things because it sounds good. I have actually done some of these things with my ex-husband, so I speak from personal experience, which is always the best teacher.

It is certainly awkward for everyone at first, and the kids will wonder if this means that you will be getting back together. Be honest with them from the very beginning so that they do not get the wrong message. Once you have put an effort into these things, your attitude will begin to change and soften. If you can be the bigger person and let the past go, focus on the present, and determine how to empower your children's future, you will be impacting their lives positively forever.

Of course, we must always use wisdom in these circumstances. If, for instance, you have remarried and your new partner is not okay with you spending time with your ex-spouse. You can come up with some ideas that will fit into your own situation. If spending time together is simply out of the question, do not feel guilty about that. You can still make efforts to speak positively about your children's father, which will earn your children's respect, something we mothers work hard to achieve.

# THE NON-CUSTODIAL MOTHERS

I know the road you walk on—I have worn your shoes for many years and I know, firsthand, the heaviness, guilt, and remorse a mom feels when she cannot kiss her children goodnight or snuggle them to sleep or hear about their day at school. While this is a weight that is much too heavy for any mother to carry, I have good news. You don't have to carry it anymore. Put it down.

I will share a very personal secret with you, because I care deeply about you and the walls of pain which threaten to close in and suffocate you. My three sons and I lived in a very comfortable little town where the people were friendly, caring, and there was a general calm. The schools were excellent, with the high school being a small private Christian academy where the teachers actually cared about the kids.

My oldest son was turning fourteen years old and just finishing up his last month of junior high. He was a popular boy, on every sports team imaginable, and I was so looking forward to his little graduation into high school. High school promised to be full of potential.

I picked him up at lunch in late May, and as we were sitting there pigging out on subs and soda pop, he blurted out, "Mom, I want to live with dad so that I can go to a big high school in the fall." I nearly threw up. His father lived an hour away. I calmly told him that we would certainly talk about it, and thanked him for telling me, but he had to get back to class.

Somehow, I managed to keep myself composed while I drove him back to his school and he got out. I waved and suddenly realized that this scene would not be replayed again. I quickly drove home, got myself inside, locked the door, and broke. I determined to fight this move with all I had (which was not much by this time). When my son came home that afternoon, we spoke about it, we argued about it, we cried about it, and finally he looked me right in the eyes and said, "I am fourteen years old and nobody should have the right to tell me that I cannot live with whichever of my parents I choose to live with." I had to agree and assured him that I would respect his decision, as long as he thought it through very thoroughly prior to making the final decision.

August came and my son's father came to pick him up. My son had a small duffle bag and a box ready to go. He kissed me and said, "I love you, mom." And with that, he and his father each picked up a box and were gone.

My precious firstborn child has now graduated and is doing wonderfully. I am so very proud of him and he knows it because I tell him. However, I missed a large portion of his life. I missed having him come home his first day of high school and rambling off all the events of the day. I missed him trying out for hockey and I missed his excitement when his name was on the roster.

I watched his brothers miss him like crazy and for weeks I would set a place for him at the table. I'm sure you know what I mean. His room was absolutely off-limits to everyone and I was not able to even open his door for months. He did come back to visit often, and I spent much time driving to watch his sports and just to take him for supper or a movie, but it was not the same.

My son lived elsewhere and it threatened to kill me. Believe me when I tell you, if you live without your children, I understand and thoroughly empathize with you. Nobody—absolutely nobody—can even begin to understand the weight of pain that comes with being the non-custodial parent.

With that piece of my life open for you to see, let me add this— there are so many ways to keep in connection with your children when they don't live under your roof. I had to come up with specific and concrete things I could do to ensure the connection did not get damaged.

One of the most important things that we can do for our children is to support them. I did not care much for his father at that time, but the truth was that he remained my son's father—nothing was ever going to change that. I had to realize that I had a choice. I could either support my son's decision and continue to build a solid, respectful relationship with him or I could absolutely fight it and in doing so drive a wedge between us. I was not willing to do that.

Supporting such a decision requires grace. Much grace. It means smiling when you want to cry and being strong when you want to break. You do these things for your kid's best interest. You see, being a mom means overlooking our own selfish wants and desires to do what is the best thing for our children. Does that mean that I thought it best for my son to leave my home and go live with his father? Absolutely not, no parent does. However, it was best for my son to know that he was not a pawn, not a prize, but a child with two parents who loved him. It was in his best interest to know that even if his mother was sad, she would rise above her own desires to put the needs of her children first. My son has since thanked me and acknowledged his respect for me.

You cannot fake support. It must be real and genuine and from the heart, because if it is not, your children will know you are faking, which means you are not really supporting them. You must find somewhere in your heart where it is okay for your children to love their father, and you must be able to demonstrate that to them.

Once you do so, your life will become much simpler—not necessarily less painful, but simpler.

There are countless ways you can stay in a daily relationship with your children even if you only see them once a month or every other weekend. I text my children almost to the point of being annoying. Every morning I send them a "Good morning, sunshine" message and every night I send them a "Good night" message. The specific messages may not mean much or have sweetness or lovely words attached, but it is the message itself that means something. My sons know that I think of them every morning and every night—that they are on my heart and in my mind always.

One thing that seems to make an impact is to actually ask your children what it is that you can do to let them know they are loved. I spoke to each of my sons separately and had them make a list of things that I could do that would allow them to know that I love them deeply and that no matter how many miles might separate us, they are absolutely deeply valued by their mom.

They each made a list of numerous specific things that would empower them with the knowledge of being valued and loved. What I found very surprising is that, while their lists overlapped slightly, they each had very different things listed. This told me that they each feel love in a different way. Some of their items were a bit difficult to accomplish, but other things were very simple and could be easily done every single day.

My oldest son said simply, "Tell me you love me with words— just say *I love you*." How simple is that? When he turned eighteen, I could not be there. However, I did one simple act and he knew, deep in his heart, that he was incredibly valued. I ordered a pizza and had the pizza shop deliver it to my son's work with a note scribbled inside the pizza box, under the pizza, that said, "Enjoy your birthday, son… I love you… Mom."

It didn't even take the pizza guy much persuading to have him scribble that on the box before he put the pizza in. That way, it was like a puzzle—with each piece of pizza my son (and his work buddies) ate, he got another few letters to his message. He phoned me before the pizza was even half gone to thank me and I could tell from his voice that he knew his mom loved him.

There are emails and handwritten letters and little objects that can be mailed. My sons all love getting little packages in the mail from me. Whether it's a t-shirt I thought they might like, or a few bucks, or just a little note with words of encouragement scribbled on it, they know from these tiny little gestures that they are absolutely loved.

## A Little Support Makes Their World Go Round

It seems crazy for me to say, "Support your kids." I can hear you screaming at the top of your lungs, "I support my kids every single month when I write that big fat check to their father." That is not the support I am speaking of.

Emotionally support your children. It is ridiculously difficult to do when you want them in your home and under your care. It seems nearly inconceivable at times when they phone you crying that they miss you. But take heart—it is not impossible. The Lord promises us that we can do all things through Christ's strength, and indeed if you find your strength in Him, you can do whatever is necessary to emotionally support your children, even though your own emotions may be shattering beneath you.

If your kids get emotional when they leave your house or when you leave them after the weekend, you will know how very difficult such a transition is. You are an adult and have skills to deal with such things. You may break inside as you walk away for another week or two, or maybe longer, but you can see beyond this moment. You know how fast time flies and that you will be okay. Imagine for a moment, your child trying to figure out how to cope when it is you that is crying or being overly emotional.

Children do not want to see their moms sad or teary eyed or sobbing every time they must return to their fathers. Kids want to protect their moms, so imagine how difficult it must be when they see you, their mom, broken and crying and knowing they can do nothing to help. These children do not have the maturity or coping mechanisms in place to deal with such pain and they internalize that pain, blaming themselves. They are seemingly powerless, but we can empower our children in such circumstances.

Perhaps we don't have what we want—our children—but they do not have what they want—their families. We often forget that it is not about us and we overlook their tears and brokenness and say, "Well, if only your father were not so selfish" or "Well your dad is being so stubborn or uncooperative." We sometimes get even meaner and say things like, "Your dad doesn't even really want you—he just doesn't want me to have you."

When my youngest son was living with his father, this precious boy often wanted to live with his mom. For reasons that only God knows, he continued to live with his father. I chose not to fight in the court systems for this boy to live with me, because I have seen those battles and in the end, regardless of the legal outcome, the child always loses. There are no winners in those battles.

I chose instead to love my son by emotionally supporting him right where he was. His father genuinely loves him and my son was not in danger by being there. While his father may not have parented him like I would have, or thought best, he parented him and my son did fine. My son always had his own room in my home and when the day came that he was old enough to make his own choice and say he was going to live with mom, he had a place— his own place.

When my son would phone me sobbing so hard and the only words he could get out were "I miss you," I had a choice. I could easily have started blasting his father, reminding him that the only reason he wasn't with me was because his father was being selfish (that was my opinion), or I could support and love my son. I chose the latter. I would sing to him and many times we would watch a basketball or football game over the telephone and often I would read the bible to him over the phone.

By doing these things, my son learned that he could be sad and share his feelings and be secure that I would just listen and love him rather than start berating his father. After all, just because he wanted to live with his mom did not mean he did not dearly love his dad.

If, on the other hand, I would have made the other choice and began rebuking his father, he would not have felt safe to share his feelings and would have stopped altogether. Children will not continue to defend one parent to the other forever; they will just begin to disrespect and withdraw from the parent who can't control his or her mouths.

When did children become objects to fight over? I have been there, ladies—I am not judging anyone, because I am guilty of all the things I am warning you against. We are all human and we all want what we think is best for our children.

What is best for our children is to stop fighting over them. Please hear me: I know the feeling of despair when we have just spent four or five weeks of summer fun with our children. I understand the week prior to them going back to dad's and pull away from them just a wee bit—even if we think we don't. I understand pulling up to that driveway and having to give your kids that last hug, after which you know you won't be seeing them for a few weeks, or a few months, and trying to keep from falling apart right there in that driveway as their father watches out the front window. I get it. I've walked it. I have pulled away from that driveway and barely got to the next block before having to pull over because I couldn't see through my stinging wet eyes.

There is good news. I made it, and so can you. Better yet, my kids made it. Not once did they think that I didn't care about them or love them because they didn't see my tears. They saw my heart and knew that when I winked at them and walked away, it was so they didn't see me break. By finding my strength in Christ, I was able to empower my children to enjoy their lives and be kids rather than worry about mom.

So can you. Love your children by simply supporting them where they are. Smile when you feel like sulking and laugh when you feel like crying. Look up when you feel like falling down and when you think you just can't do it anymore, climb up into our Father's lap and rest in the shadow of the Almighty.

"*He who dwells in the shelter of the Most High will rest in the shadow of the Almighty. I will say of the Lord, 'He is my refuge and my fortress, my God, in whom I trust'*" (Psalm 91:1-2).

# Conclusion

Raising children alone is undoubtedly the most stretching, lonely, exhausting, and unappreciated role any woman will ever play. There are certainly not enough resources available, and if there were, we would not have the time to take advantage of them.

I have heard many well-known people make the following statement, and I tend to absolutely agree: "Single parenting is the most difficult job on the planet." It is not "among" the most difficult, but it *is* without doubt, unequivocally, the *most* difficult. Not because it takes brute physical strength or a mind like Einstein or three degrees or unending funds. Raising kids alone takes heart, a heart that is magical—so incredibly soft and pliable, yet hard and unyielding as steel. It takes willpower to keep our emotions in check while remaining sensitive and compassionate.

It is the most difficult job because there is no equipping for such a task. The sheer responsibility of this task is overwhelming. To consider the precious little mouldable lives that God has placed in our care can cause us to feel incapable and unworthy, but God has chosen to place these babies in our care. It was neither accidental nor a coincidence. He knew what our situation would look like and in all His wisdom and knowledge, He choose us to parent these little ones.

He knows that we, His daughters, can rely on His strength to successfully accomplish the insurmountable task before us...raising His little ones.

The tools I have given you in this book are but a small scoop from God's bucket of wisdom. The answer is not this book, our own abilities, our own strength, or our own wisdom. It is God. Seek Him and ask for His wisdom and He will provide all that we need, because as much as we love and adore our children, in the end, they belong to Him—they are His children.

In order to maintain our inner joy and love our children the way they need to be loved, we must internalize the truth of who we are—and who God is. He does not intend for us to drag along, broken, hunched over, and forever disappointed—pulling behind us weights of unfairness, guilt, and loneliness. He offers so much more—we just need to take it.

He is our identity and our joy. He alone can be all that we require. He alone can provide the grace and wisdom to meet our children's needs…and our own.

It is only through Christ and His word that we will be equipped to raise a generation of excellent kids. Together, we can do it. Be blessed. Enjoy your children. Trust the Lord.